EUROPE *MADE EASY*

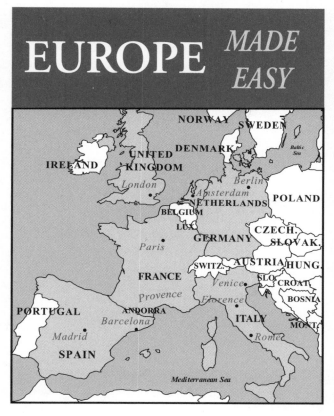

Andy Herbach

Open Road Publishing

Open Road Publishing

We offer travel guides to American and foreign locales. Our books tell it like it is, often with an opinionated edge, and our experienced authors always give you only the best information you need to have a wonderful trip – your *perfect* trip! For more information and to order any Open Road travel guide, visit: *www.openroadguides.com*.

Text and maps copyright © 2006 by Andy Herbach
ISBN 1-59360-073-9
Library of Congress Control No. 2006927492
–All Rights Reserved–

ABOUT THE AUTHOR

Andy Herbach is a lawyer and resides in Milwaukee. He is the co-author of Open Road's popular menu translators and restaurant guides: *Eating & Drinking in Paris*, *Eating & Drinking in Italy*, *Eating & Drinking in Spain* and *Eating & Drinking in Latin America*. He is also the author of *Provence Made Easy*, *Amsterdam Made Easy*, *Berlin Made Easy*, and *Paris Made Easy*. You can e-mail him corrections, additions, and comments at eatndrink@aol.com or through his website at www.eatndrink.com.

Updates to this guide can be found on the message board at www.eatndrink.com.

TABLE OF CONTENTS

Maps

ACKNOWLEDGMENTS

The Rome and Florence chapters were written by Doug Morris.
The London chapter was written by Paul Tarrant.
English editors: Jonathan Stein and (except Florence) Marian Olson
French editor: Mary Fossier
German editor: Professor Robert Jamison
Amsterdam, Barcelona, Berlin, Provence, Madrid and Paris maps from designmaps.com.
Web sites: www.eatndrink.com and www.openroadguides.com
Contributor: Karl Raaum
Additional research: Mark Berry, Jeff Kurz, Jim Mortell, Dan Schmidt, and Trish and Terry Medalen

INTRODUCTION

Europe has so much to offer. If art is your passion, there's the Louvre in Paris, the world's largest—and greatest—art museum. If eating and drinking in a festive atmosphere is more to your liking, you've got Madrid's *tapas* bars. And if you're a history buff, you can take a thought-provoking stroll along what was the Berlin Wall.

As the title says, our little guide will make your trip easy. Tuck it into your pocket and head out for a great day of sightseeing. You'll have access to Europe's top sights right at your fingertips (from the canals of Venice to the Sistine Chapel in Rome to the Picasso Museum in Barcelona to the Red-Light District in Amsterdam), with insider tips on cafes, restaurants, shops, and where to sample delicious European wines. We've also given detailed directions for walks of the major sights of some of Europe's most spectacular cities.

If you have only a few days, we'll make it easy for you to truly experience Europe. Our walks are designed for you to see the most sights in the shortest time. So forget those large, bulky travel tomes. This handy little pocket guide to Europe is all you need to make your visit enjoyable, memorable—*and easy.*

BARCELONA

Cosmopolitan Barcelona is the gateway to Spain's Mediterranean coast. You'll find world-class museums, including the Museu Picasso, with some of this artist's most interesting works. Or perhaps you'd prefer to wander the narrow streets of the Barri Gòtic (Gothic Quarter) filled with medieval buildings. Barcelona also has some of the most interesting architecture in Europe, especially those structures designed by Antoni Gaudí. Don't miss the indescribable and uncompleted La Sagrada Familia (Church of the Holy Family), Barcelona's most recognizable landmark. And get ready to stay up late in Spain's second largest city, because Barcelona is known for its pulsating nightlife.

La Sagrada Familia
Plaça de la Sagrada Familia/401
Carrer de Mallorca
Tel. 93/2073031
Open daily Apr-Sep 9am-8pm;
Oct-Mar 9am-6pm
Admission: €8 (€2 for the tower elevator)
Metro: Sagrada Familia
www.sagradafamilia.org

The foundation stone of Barcelona's most recognizable landmark was laid in 1882. Antoni Gaudí, the famous Catalan architect, was tragically killed in an accident before he could complete this architectural masterpiece. The roofless Church of the Holy Family looks like some huge melting sand castle. Gaudí is buried in the crypt (where there's a museum showing how he intended the building to look upon its completion). The elevator trip (or steps) to the top of the towers is not for those afraid of heights. You just can't come to Barcelona and not visit this indescribable building: Weird, majestic, eclectic and awe-inspiring, all at the same time!

Museu Picasso
(Picasso Museum)
15-23 Carrer Montcada
Tel. 93/3196310
Open Tue-Sat 10am-8pm, Sun 10am-3pm
Admission: €5
Metro: Jaume I
www.museupicasso.bcn.es

The largest collection of art by Pablo Picasso (all 3,600 of them) is at this museum housed in adjoining Gothic palaces. The museum focuses on his early years (he lived in Barcelona from the age of 14 to 21). Especially interesting is room 11 containing the depressing and bleak works from his "Blue Period." A must for those interested in this fascinating artist.

Park Güell
Carrer d'Olot
Tel. 93/2193811
Open daily 9am-8pm (until 6pm in winter)
Admission: Free (Museum: €4)
Metro: Lesseps (then a steep uphill walk) or take bus #24 from Plaça de Catalunya or the red tourist bus

The two gatehouses to this park look like gingerbread houses from a book of fairy tales. From the ceramic decorated entrance to the wrought-iron lampposts to the park benches, this incredible place allows you to experience Gaudí's

Restaurant Tips

EL XAMPANYET
22 Carrer Montcada
93/3197003
Closed Mon, Tue and Sun (dinner)
Metro: Jaume I
A *Xampanyeria* is a bar found in and around Barcelona serving *cava* (sparkling wine). This popular, blue-tiled bar is a great place for a quick bite while visiting the Picasso Museum. Inexpensive.

TÈXTIL CAFÉ
12-14 Carrer Montcada (near the Picasso Museum)
Tel. 93/2682598
Open daily 10am-midnight
Metro: Jaume I
Have lunch (pasta dishes, salads and sandwiches) on the terrace of the gorgeous palace that houses the Textile Museum. Moderate.

brilliance as a landscape designer. There are excellent views from the pavilion. You can visit **Casa Museu Gaudí**, the home where Gaudí lived from 1906 to 1926, containing some of his

drawings and personal belongings. Today, the park is the place to come to enjoy the quirkiness of Gaudí and Barcelona; it's unlike any other in Europe. Visit the gift shop for some fun stuff.

La Barceloneta/Port Olímpic
Along the shore, south of Parc de la Ciutadella
Metro: Barceloneta or Ciutadella

La Barceloneta (Little Barcelona) is a quaint neighborhood of narrow streets with hanging laundry and palm tree-lined promenades along the shore. The beach stretches for 2.5 miles. You can stroll to the Port Olímpic (Olympic Port) one mile away, where there are lots of cafés, beach bars (*xiringuitos*), clubs and a casino. Overlooking it all is a giant copper goldfish sculpture by Frank Gehry in front of the Hotel Arts.

LA RAMBLA WALK
Metro: Catalunya

A walk down La Rambla is a must for all visitors to Barcelona. Highlights: **Museu d'Art Contemporani de Barcelona, Mercat de la Boqueria,** and **Monument a Colom.** Approximate distance: one mile. See map on pages 10-11. Note that the Mercat de la Boqueria is closed on Sundays.

To begin your walk, take the metro to the Catalunya stop.

You begin at the large square, Plaça de Catalunya, and begin your trek down to the port.

Be warned that Barcelona is notorious for pickpockets. Be extra careful near tourist attractions, especially along La Rambla.

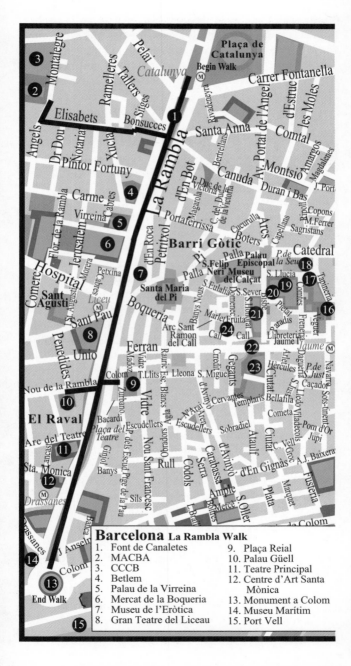

Barcelona La Rambla Walk

1. Font de Canaletes
2. MACBA
3. CCCB
4. Betlem
5. Palau de la Virreina
6. Mercat de la Boqueria
7. Museu de l'Eròtica
8. Gran Teatre del Liceau
9. Plaça Reial
10. Palau Güell
11. Teatre Principal
12. Centre d'Art Santa Mònica
13. Monument a Colom
14. Museu Marítim
15. Port Vell

Eixample

Urquinaona

R. Lluria

Bruc

Girona

Ausiàs

Baile

Saint Joan

Laietana

Urquinaona

Jonqueres

Trafalgar

Ronda de Sant Pere

Ali

Ortigosa

Manufactures

Trafalgar

Méndez Núñez

Trafalgar

St. Benet

Arc de Triomf

Palau de la Música Catalana

Amadeu Vives

Sant Mes Alt

de Deu del Pilar

Bou de St. Pere

Argenter

Monec

Sert

Victoria

Plaça de Sant Pere

Arc de Triomf

Beates

Verdaguer i Cal

Sant Pere Mitja

Laietana

Sant Pere Mes

Castro

Freixures

Jaume Giralt

Metges

B. de S. Pere

Sequia

Llàstics

Cortines

Portal Nou

Petons

F. Cambó

Mercaders

Tragí

La Ribera

Gombau

Tarròs

Fonollar

Montanyans

Vermell

Tiradors

Tantarantana

Comerç

Passieg de Picasso

Massanet

Mercat Santa Caterina

Pellisser

Lliri

Jacint

Corders

S.Cugat

Blanqueria

Allada

Gallifa

S.Silv

Oli

Sidé

Semolers

Assaonadors

Museu de la Xocolata

Boria

Ciutat

Boquer

Candeles

Princessa

Princessa

Cotoners

Barra de Ferro

Cremat Gran

Fusina

Vigatans

Girtu

Grunyl

Barra

Museu Tèxtil

25

Galeria

Sabateret

Comerç

Comercial

Mercantil

Argenteria

Brosoli

Rosic

Museu Maeght

Crera

Rec

Manresa

Mirallers

Barbier-Mueller

Seca

Basea

Vella

Montcada

Mosques

Born

Rec

Antic de S. Joan

Ribera

Parc de la Citadella

Nau

Abaixad

Sombrerers

S. Maria del Mar

Santa Maria

Espart.

Calders

Comerç

J. Massana

Canv. Nous

Can. Vella

Ases

Espaseria

Bonaire

Guillem

Pescateria

Agullers

Malculnat

Rera Palau

Consol. de Mar

Argentera

Laietana

Isabel II

If you like to shop, pop into the giant department store **El Corte Inglés** on the square at 14 Plaça de Catalunya. This is *the* department store in Barcelona and all of Spain. In addition to clothing and household goods, check out the supermarket on the lower level and the café/restaurant on the seventh floor. Closed Sundays.

Head to the pedestrian walkway La Rambla. Walk down the middle of the street. This section of the street is called Rambla de Canaletes after the fountain Font de Canaletes located here.

On your right at the beginning of the walk (near #129) is a lamppost with a drinking fountain at its base. It's said that if you drink from the fountain **Font de Canaletes**, you're guaranteed to return to Barcelona.

All along La Rambla, you'll see crowds of people gathering around street performers. Devils, mimes (unfortunately), and, if you're lucky, the old bald guy with goofy glasses stroking his guitar and playing a Pan flute with his Chihuahua in matching goofy glasses by his side.

Now continue walking down La Rambla. Turn right at number 121 La Rambla (there's an old-fashioned pharmacy on the corner) onto Carrer del Bonsuccés.

Walk through the Plaça del Bonsuccés. The street turns into Carrer Elisabets (check out the old herb store at number 2).

You'll run into the street Carrer dels Àngels. To your right (that white building) is the **Museu d'Art Contemporani de Barcelona** (Museum of Contemporary Art), also called MACBA. Housed in a building that is a work of art itself, this museum features contemporary works by Spanish, Catalan and international artists. *Tel. 93/4120810. Open Mon, Wed-Fri 11am-8pm (only until 7:30pm Oct-May), Sat 10am-8pm, Sun 10am-3pm. Admission: €6. Metro: Universitat or Catalunya. www.macba.es.*

Behind MACBA is the **Centre de Cultura Contemporània de Barcelona** (CCCB) (Center of Contemporary Culture of

Barcelona). There are changing exhibits at this cultural center housed in the Casa de la Caritat, a former almshouse dating back to the 1800s.

Retrace you steps to La Rambla, and continue down the street. This section is called Rambla dels Estudis.

At number 115, you'll pass by a market filled with shops selling all sorts of pets, especially birds and fish.

On your right (at the corner of Carrer del Carme) is the Baroque exterior of the church **Betlem** (the interior dates back only to the 1930s because of a fire). On the next block down La Rambla (on your right at number 99) is the **Palau de la Virreina**. It has a fantastic Baroque and Rococo interior that you can see as part of the cultural department's changing exhibits. If you want, you can pop into its courtyard. If you're lucky, they will have the *gegants* out. They're 16-foot-tall fiberglass statues that are used in festivals and parades. A great photo opportunity.

Continue down La Rambla. This section of the street is called Rambla de Sant Josep.

Right after number 91 (on your right) you'll reach **Mercat de la Boqueria**. Pass through the iron gateway to one of the largest, most interesting and colorful markets in Europe. You'll find everything from fresh produce to delicious snacks under its wrought iron-and-glass roof. Each stall in the market is numbered. My favorite is the counter of **El Quim** at numbers 584-585. It's a great place for a drink and *tapas*. Closed Sundays.

After visiting the market, continue down La Rambla.

Across from the market at number 96 is the **Museu de l'Eròtica** housing over 800 pieces of erotic art from the Middle Ages to today. *Tel. 93/3189865. Open June-Sep 10am-midnight, Oct-May 11am-9pm. Admission: €8. Metro: Liceu. www.erotica-museum.com.*

On the right at number 83 (at the corner of Carrer de la Petxina) check out the beautiful mosaic façade and the fantastic sweets (especially the chocolates!) at Escribà (open daily 8:30am-9pm), an Art Nouveau eatery dating back to the early 1900s.

Admire the interesting façade of the building at number 77 on the right. It's covered with Art Nouveau mosaics.

Look for the mosaic set into the sidewalk by abstract artist Joan Miró at Plaça de la Boqueria. You're about halfway through your walk.

Continue down La Rambla. This section is called Rambla dels Caputxins.

On your right, at the corner of Carrer de Sant Pau, is the renovated opera house Gran Teatre del Liceu, parts of which date back to 1848.

Detour

On the left side of the street is Carrer de la Boqueria. This will take you into the narrow streets of the Barri Gòtic (Gothic Quarter) filled with medieval buildings.

Guided tours of the hall, Room of Mirrors and marble foyer are daily at 10am for €6 (shorter tours at 11:30am, noon and 1pm for €4).

On the left side of the street is the famous Café de l'Opera at number 74.

If you cross the street to the left side, you can visit one of the loveliest squares in all of Europe (entry through Carrer de Colom).

At number 46, head into the square Plaça Reial. This lovely square, with the Fountain of Three Graces, is filled with palm trees, cafés, shops and bars. A great place for a break. Check out those interesting lampposts designed by Gaudí (notice the winged dragons perched on top with their tails wrapped around the posts).

Now head back to La Rambla and cross the street.

Right after the Hotel Oriente, turn right on Carrer Nou de la Rambla. You'll see Gaudí's incredible Palau Güell (at number 3-5) (one-hour guided visits only, for €3). As you approach, look up to your left at the chimney and ventilator shafts covered with colorful and ornate tile patterns.

You've now entered El Raval. It's an ethnically diverse neighborhood where you must be careful, especially at night, as this is a favorite haunt of pickpockets and prostitutes. It's not nearly as bad as it's been in the past, but still be careful.

Now head back to La Rambla and continue walking toward the port.

On your right at number 27, just after the Carrer de l'Arc del Teatre, is the curvy façade of the theater, Teatre Principal, which dates back to the mid-1800s.

Continue down La Rambla. This section is called Rambla de Santa Mònica. You'll find portrait artists and local art for sale here.

At number 7 are the cloister and tower of the Centre d'Art Santa Mònica, a former convent dating back to the early 1600s. It's now a cultural center with changing exhibits.

That huge monument at the port is the Monument a Colom (Columbus Monument) honoring the famous explorer from where it is said he was welcomed home in 1492. You can take an elevator to the top for great views (€2.20).

An interesting end to your walk is to take a *golondrina*, one of the boats docked here at the Port de la Pau. These boats provide excellent views of the city's coast. They depart to the breakwater (35-minute trip, €4) or to the Port Olímpic (a two-hour journey, €9).

Also at the **Port Vell** (Old Port) is the **Museu Marítim** (Maritime Museum) housed in the **Drassanes Reials** (Royal Shipyards), tracing the history of the Catalans' reliance upon the sea. A historic 1918 sailing ship, the Santa Eulàlia, is docked in the harbor across the street. A must for sea lovers. *Tel. 93/3429929. Open daily 10am-7pm (closed Mon in winter). Admission: €6. Metro: Drassanes. www.diba.es/mmaritim.*

Cross the footbridge here and you'll find the **L'Aquàrium**, part of the **Maremàgnum** entertainment complex. This large aquarium is home to 8,000 fish in 21 tanks, including a huge shark tunnel that kids love. *Tel. 93/2217474. Open Jul and Aug daily 9:30am-11pm, Sep and weekends 9:30am-9:30pm, rest of the year 9:30am-9pm, admittance until one hour before closing. Admission: €14. Metro: Drassanes. www.aquariumbcn.com.* And here ends our Rambla walk!

Barri Gòtic
(Gothic Quarter)
Metro: Jaume I

Explore the narrow streets and lovely squares of Europe's best-preserved medieval quarter. It's home to the following sights:

The **Museu d'Història de la Ciutat** (Museum of the History of the City) contains the largest underground excavation of any European city. You'll walk on glass ramps to view the remains of the Roman town of Barcino. You'll also have access to the beautiful **Saló del Tinell**, a banquet hall dating back to the 14th century. It was here that Columbus was received upon his return from America. *Tel. 93/3151111. Carrer del Veguer. Open Oct-May Tue-Sat 10am-2pm and 4pm-8pm, Sun 10am-3pm; June-Sep Tue-Sat 10am-8pm, Sun 10am-3pm. Admission: €4. www.museuhistoria.bcn.es.*

The Museu Frederic Marès (Museum Frederic Mares) is located in an impressive Romanesque and Gothic palace. This museum (named after a Spanish sculptor) houses sculpture from pre-Roman times to the 20th century. It's also home to the Museu Sentimental, an interesting collection of household items from the past four centuries. *Carrer dels Comtes. Tel. 93/3105800. Open Tue-Sat 10am-7pm, Sun 10am-3pm. Admission: €3. www.museumares.bcn.es.*

Devotees of religious art shouldn't miss the Museu Diocesà (Diocesan Museum). *Plaça de la Seu. Tel. 93/3152213. Open Tue-Sat 10am-2pm and 5pm-8pm, Sun 11am-2pm. Admission: €4.*

Construction on Barcelona's massive Catedral (Cathedral) began in the 13th century. It's a splendid example of Catalonian Gothic architecture, and features sculpted choir stalls dating back to the 14th century. The Sala Capitular (Chapter House) is home to a museum of medieval art. The roof (when open) has great views of the Barri Gòtic. The cathedral's beautiful and serene cloister is filled with palm trees and magnolias. Notice the 13 geese here; they're in memory of St. Eulàlia, the patron saint of the city. She was a 13-year-old who was tortured by the Romans 13 times for refusing to renounce Christianity. The geese also acted as guards by honking if someone entered. Their descendants still do lots of honking today!

The cloister is lined with chapels. You can buy a candle at the small booth at the entry. Notice that Saint Rita's chapel has the most candles, not just because it's near the entry, but because she is the patron saint of desperate, seemingly impossible causes and situations. *Plaça de la Seu. Tel. 93/3151554. Cathedral: Open daily 8am-1:30pm and 4:30pm-*

Entertainment Tip

The *sardana,* a colorful Catalonian folk dance, is performed every Sunday at noon (and some Saturdays at 6pm) in front of the cathedral.

7:30pm. Cloister: Open daily 9am-1pm and 5pm-7pm. Museum: Open daily 10am-1pm and 5:15pm-7pm. Metro: Jaume I. Admission: Free to cathedral except €2 between 1:30pm-5pm Museum: €1.50, €2 each to the choir stalls, roof and Chapter House. www.catedralbcn.org.

The square Plaça Sant Jaume is home to the government buildings for Barcelona (Ajuntament) and Catalonia (Generalitat).

Carrer del Call is the main street of the Call (the old Jewish Quarter). Here you can wander through narrow streets and small, secluded squares.

Eixample
North of Plaça de Catalunya
Metro: Passeig de Gràcia or Diagonal

Eixample means "extension." This was the modern town of Barcelona, and it was built on a grid pattern in the late 19th century. Great shopping here. Barcelona is famous for its architecture, especially those buildings of the Modernista movement (*Modernisme*), the Art Nouveau style unique to the region that flourished from 1890-1920. Chief among the architects was Antoni Gaudí. His innovative creations can be found throughout this city. We'll visit two streets in this area.

Eixample/
Sagrada Familia
1. Casa de les Punxes
2. Casa Comalat
3. Casa Milà (La Pedrera)
4. Casa Quadras
5. Fundació Antoni Tàpies
6. Manzana de la Discòrdia
7. Sagrada Familia

Passeig de Gràcia
Metro: Passeig de Gràcia

The fantastic block between Carrer Consell de Cent and Carrer Aragó is nicknamed Manzana de la Discòrdia (Block of Discord) because the buildings seemed to be trying to outdo one another.

At number 35 of Passeig de Gràcia is the Casa Lleó-Morera, designed in 1906 by Domènech i Montaner. The exterior is covered with balconies and carved floral designs, with a rooftop garden and unusual tower.

Notice the interesting *Modernisme* lampposts along the street.

At number 39 is the Museu del Perfum (Perfume Museum) with a collection of 5,000 perfume vessels, including flasks from ancient Greece, a bottle designed by Dalí, and one owned by Marie Antoinette. *Tel. 93/2160121. Open Mon-Fri 10:30am-1:30pm and 4:30pm-8pm, Sat 11am-2pm. Admission: €5. www.museodelperfume.com.*

At number 41 is Casa Amatller, dating back to 1900. Its interesting mixture of wrought iron, sculptures and ceramics was designed by Puig i Cadafalch. Its interior is Gothic Revival (which you can see only by appointment).

At number 43 is the Casa Batlló by Gaudí. You have to see it to understand how unique it is. It dates back to 1905, and its wavy façade of stone, iron and tiles is extraordinary. You can pop inside and take a look at the equally interesting interior. The roof has fascinating twisted tile chimneys. *Tel. 93/2160306. Open daily 9am-8pm. Admission: €10 (€16 includes access to the roof). www.casabatllo.es*

Around the corner at 255 Carrer d'Aragó is the Fundació Antoni Tàpies. This iron-and-brick building dates back to the 1880s. It contains a collection of the Catalan artist's mostly Abstract Expressionist works. Notice his huge sculpture on the roof. *Tel. 93/4870315. Open Tue-Sun 10am-8pm. Admission: €5. www.fundaciotapies.org.*

At number 92 Passeig de Gràcia is **Casa Milà** (La Pedrera): Is this building melting? From the unbelievable exterior to the Art Nouveau apartment to the bizarre chimneys, this great work by Gaudí is a must. It's called La Pedrera, which means "The Stone Quarry." *Tel. 90/2400973. Open daily 10am-8pm. Admission: Free to the exterior and courtyard. Interior: €8, guided tours in English Mon-Fri at 4pm.*

Entertainment Tip

In the summer, you can attend a concert on the roof of Casa Milà and sip *cava* (Spanish sparkling wine). *Tel. 90/2400973. Fri and Sat €10. Reservations required.* If you just want to try Spanish wines, head down Carrer de Provença to Vinoteca, a wine bar and wine store at number 169. *Tel. 93/4677023. Open Mon-Fri 10am-2pm and 4:30pm-8:30pm, Sat 10:30am-2pm and 5pm-8:30pm.*

Avinguda Diagonal
Metro: Avinguda Diagonal

At 442 is **Casa Comalat** by Valeri i Pupurull. Notice the twelve curved stone balconies and elaborate wrought-iron railings. If you view the building from the rear (at 316 Carrer de Còrsega), you'll see a totally different-looking building with bulging shutters.

On the other side of the street (just before Carrer de Pau Claris) is the first of two works by architect Puig i Cadafalch. At number 373 is the **Casa Quadras**, built in 1904 and featuring a St. George-slaying-a-dragon theme and beautiful stained glass. Cross the street if you want to see the detail. It houses the **Casa Asia**, an Asian cultural center with changing exhibits devoted to Asian art and history.

If you want to take a break, head into **Bar Mut**, a wine and *tapas* bar at 192 Carrer de Pau Claris near the corner of Avinguda Diagonal.

You can't miss the towers at numbers 416-420. Those towers give the **Casa de les Punxes** (House of the Spikes) its nickname (its formal name is Casa Terrades). It's another work by architect Puig i Cadafalch and dates back to 1903.

Montjuïc
(Mount of the Jews)
You can view music and lights shows at the fountain every thirty minutes May-Sep Thu-Sun 8pm-midnight, Oct-Apr Fri and Sat 7pm-9pm. Several outdoor escalators make the walk more tolerable. The blue tourist bus also stops here. Bus number 55 runs through the park.

Shopping Tip

At 85 Carrer de Roger Llúria is a great place to stock up on local food specialties. The deli/grocery J Murrià has been run by the same family since the early 1900s. Go on, try something interesting and delicious!

Metro: Espanya. Then you'll walk (uphill) for about 10 minutes and pass the Art Deco Font Màgica (Magic Fountain).

There are several sights to visit on this large hill overlooking the city center, including **Olympic Stadium**, **Poble Espanyol** (a fake and touristy Spanish village), and public gardens. Two of the museums here are:

Museu Nacional d'Art de Catalunya (MNAC): Catalan National Art Museum in the huge **Palau Nacional** (National Palace) with one of the world's finest collections of Romanesque and Early Gothic art. Closed Mondays.

Fundació Joan Miró: thousands of works by Joan Miró, one of Spain's greatest painters, known for his vibrant colors and abstract art. Closed Mondays.

BARCELONA GETTING THERE/GETTING AROUND
Pick up a free map of the city (or a larger, more detailed one for €1) and a brochure on public transportation at the tourist information offices in terminals A and B of the airport. There are also tourist offices at city hall at Plaça de Sant Jaume in the Barri Gòtic, or at the office at Plaça de Catalunya.

When you arrive at Barcelona's El Prat de Llobregat Airport, you can either take a taxi into town (about €30) or the **Aerobús** for €4 (in the arrivals lobby, you buy the ticket on the bus) to the Plaça de Catalunya (with stops at Plaça d'Espanya, Carrer Urgell and Plaça Universitat) and then take the metro to your hotel. The trip takes 35-45 minutes (depending on traffic). The bus operates 6am to midnight weekdays and 6:30am to midnight on weekends (departs at least four times per hour). To return to the airport, catch the Aerobús in front of the El Corte Inglés department store on Plaça de Catalunya (weekdays 5:30am to 11:15pm, weekends 6am to 11:15pm). Trains leave the airport train station two times per hour between 6:13am and 11:40pm for €2.25 (with stops at Sants, Plaça de Catalunya, Arc de Triomf and Clot-Aragó). Return trains leave the Plaça de Catalunya two times per hour between 5:30am and 10pm.

Once in the city, think about hopping on and off the double-decker tourist bus (Bus Turistic). The blue route covers the Gothic Quarter and Montjuïc, and the red route covers most Gaudí architectural sights and most of northern Barcelona. Public transportation is easy to use. You'll use the same ticket for bus, metro, tram or local train: Single ticket is €1.15, ten-trip ticket is €6.30. Don't forget to validate the ticket before you get on. If you're caught without a valid ticket, you'll pay a €40 fine.

MADRID

Madrid is Spain's capital city. It's not only located in the center of the country, it *is* the center of Spain. Although travelers come to visit Madrid's main attractions—including the fantastic Prado Museum—they soon get caught up in the city's lively nightlife. The *tapas* scene alone is worth the trip. Although you'll find plenty of new buildings, you'll also find Baroque and neo-Classical structures such as the Plaza Mayor (where it seems at times that everyone in Madrid is visiting) and the grand Palacio Real (Royal Palace).

Most of the city's main sights are within easy walking distance, making Madrid a visitor-friendly place. We'll discover the best sights of Madrid on two walks.

MAJOR SIGHTS WALK I
Highlights: Palacio Real, Catedral de la Almudena, and Plaza Mayor. See map on page 24. Approximate distance one mile.

Take the metro to the Ópera stop. When you exit, you'll be in the square Plaza de Isabel II. The large building here is the back of the Royal Theater. Facing the Royal Theater, head left to the street Calle de Vergara. Turn right onto Calle de Vergara and then right onto Calle de Carlos III and head into the large square.

This square is the Plaza de Oriente. It's lined with statues of the kings and queens of Spain (that's Philip IV on his horse in the center of the square).

On one side of the square is the Teatro Real (Royal Theater). It was built in 1850 and is the site of opera and ballet performances, but the real star is the interior of the building itself. There are guided tours Monday, Tuesday, Thursday and Friday from 11am to 1pm, and Saturday and Sunday 11am to 1:30pm. A 50-minute tour is €4 and a 30-minute "*rapida*" tour is €2.

That huge building on the square is our next sight.

Perched on a hill overlooking the city, the Palacio Real (Royal Palace) has 3,000 rooms, and some are open to the public. Spaniards will proudly tell you that it's twice as large as Buckingham Palace. You can visit the rooms of King Alfonso XIII, who was the last resident until he abdicated in 1931.

The present building dates back to 1738, and is built on the sight of a former Moorish fortress. Also, don't miss the Painting Gallery (filled with pieces by such notables as Velázquez and Goya), the Throne Room, the Reception Room and the Royal Armoury. The elaborate Changing of the Guard takes place in the courtyard at noon on the first

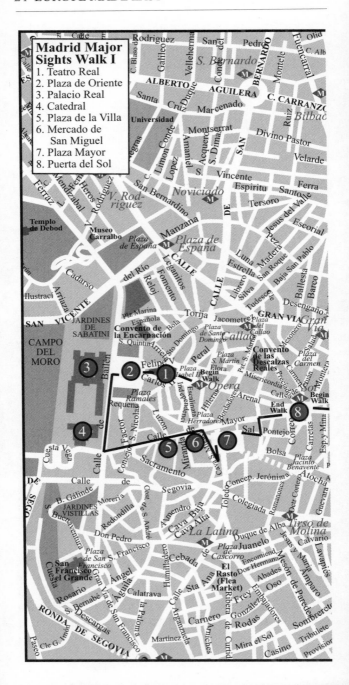

Madrid Major Sights Walk I
1. Teatro Real
2. Plaza de Oriente
3. Palacio Real
4. Catedral
5. Plaza de la Villa
6. Mercado de San Miguel
7. Plaza Mayor
8. Puerta del Sol

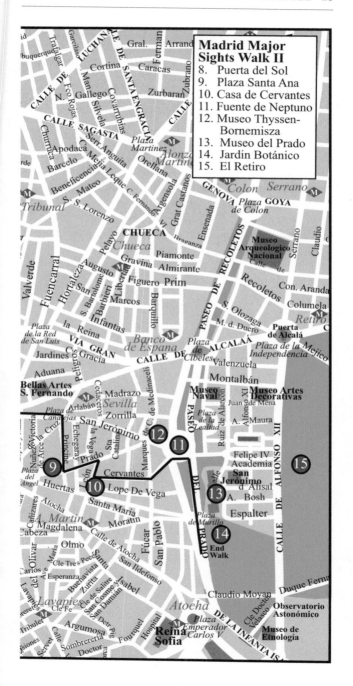

Madrid Major Sights Walk II
8. Puerta del Sol
9. Plaza Santa Ana
10. Casa de Cervantes
11. Fuente de Neptuno
12. Museo Thyssen-Bornemisza
13. Museo del Prado
14. Jardín Botánico
15. El Retiro

Wednesday of every month. *Tel. 91/4548800. Open Oct-Mar Mon-Sat 9:30am-5pm, Sun 9am-2pm, Apr-Sep Mon-Sat 9am-6pm, Sun 9am-3pm. Admission: €9. Metro: Ópera. www.patrimonionacional.es.*

With the Royal Palace to your back, head right down Calle de Bailén. To your right is our next stop, just past the Royal Palace.

Construction of the Catedral de Nuestra Señora de la Almudena began in 1883 and was not completed until 1993. Admission is free, so enter through the huge sculpted doors and look up at the colorful ceiling. In a chapel behind the altar is the empty 12th-century coffin of St. Isidro, the patron saint of Madrid. Forty years after he died, the coffin was opened (now, who decided to do this?) and his body had not decayed, which was enough for the pope to canonize him. He's buried elsewhere in the city. *10 Calle de Bailén. Tel. 91/5422200. Open daily 10am-1:30pm and 6pm-8pm. Admission: Free. Metro: Ópera.*

Continue down Calle de Bailén until you reach Calle Mayor. Take a left onto Calle Mayor. Walk down the left side of the street. At Calle de la Almudena, you'll notice a bronze statue of a man looking at a glass enclosure.

The glass enclosure contains the ruins of the church Iglesia de Nuestra Señora de la Almudena.

Pass Calle de Factor and Calle de San Nicolás. At Calle de Calderón de la Barca, cross the street to the square.

You can experience a little bit of medieval times at the Plaza de la Villa. This is Madrid's oldest square, dominated by the Casa de la Villa, the former town hall (to your right). The building straight ahead is Casa de Cisneros, which dates back to 1537. To your left is the 15th-century tower Torre de los Lujanes.

Continue down Calle Mayor. Turn right at Plaza de San Miguel.

The iron-and-glass building here is the 1915 Mercado de San Miguel, filled with fresh produce, meats and lots of stinky fish.

After you've visited the market, turn right from the Plaza de San Miguel onto Cava de San Miguel.

The narrow bars that look like caves here are called *mesones*, and are an interesting place for a late-night *sangria*. This is a great area to have a drink and *tapas*.

Head down Cava de San Miguel and it turns into Calle Cuchilleros.

On the left at number 17 is Botín, made famous in Ernest Hemingway's *The Sun Also Rises*. You'll eat in tiled, wood-beamed dining rooms in Madrid's (and allegedly, the world's) oldest restaurant. It's quite touristy, but the food, especially roast suckling pig (*cochinillo assado*), won't disappoint. Stop here for a meal if you have the time. Moderate-Expensive. *Tel. 91/3664217. Open daily. Reservations required. Metro: Puerta del Sol or La Latina.*

Turn around and head back up the street to the steps leading into Madrid's grand square. On the steps up, you'll pass Las Cuevas de Luis Candelas, Madrid's oldest tavern.

The Plaza Mayor is an arcaded and cobblestone square dating back to 1617. It's surrounded by buildings with balconies and is truly the heart of Viejo Madrid (Old Madrid), and one of Europe's grandest squares. Throughout the years the square has seen everything from public executions during the Inquisition to bullfights. Notice the colorful paintings on the Casa de la Panaderia ("bakery") on the north side of the square. It remains a meeting place for all of Madrid, and is the sight of

Restaurant Tip
LAS CUEVAS DE LUIS CANDELAS
1 Calle Cuchilleros
Tel. 91/3665428
Open daily
Metro: Puerta del Sol
or La Latina
Okay, so it's touristy with its strolling musicians and host dressed like a bandit. But this "cave" off of the Plaza Mayor is the oldest tavern in Madrid. *Tapas* and dining (especially barbecued meats). Moderate-Expensive.

of frequent markets and festivals. There's a huge Christmas market here in December, and a stamp, coin and art market on Sundays from around 10am to 2pm That's Felipe III, who ordered this square to be built, on his horse in the center of the square. Take a stroll around this grand square.

You can exit the square through the northeast corner (between numbers 31 and 32) onto the street Calle de la Sal. Turn left onto Calle de Postas. You'll pass a branch of the Museo del Jamón ("Museum of Ham")–a tapas bar–on your left, and then continue on to the large square Puerta del Sol. From here you can take the Puerta del Sol metro back to your hotel, or you can continue on to our next walk.

MAJOR SIGHTS WALK II
Highlights: **Puerta del Sol, Museo del Prado** and **Parque del Retiro**. See map on page 25. Approximate distance one mile.

Take the metro to Puerta del Sol to begin this walk.

The **Puerta del Sol** (which means "Gateway of the Sun") is always crowded. There's a bronze plaque set into the sidewalk on the south side of the square from which all distances in Spain are measured. That statue is King Charles III (who ruled from 1759-1788) on his horse. He's facing a building that dates back to 1768 and is now the headquarters of Madrid's regional government. Check out the huge Tio Pepe sign, Madrid's first billboard. On the corner of Calle de Carmen is a bronze statue of a bear – the symbol of Madrid.

From the square, head east in the direction of the Tio Pepe sign (the street to the right of the Tio Pepe sign) on Carrera de San Jerónimo. Walk on the right side of the street.

At the corner of Calle Victoria is the **Museo del Jamón** at 6 Carrera de San Jerónimo. The "Museum of Ham" isn't really a museum, but a chain of delis serving and selling ham. You can't miss it, as you'll see hundreds of hams hanging from the ceiling. Try a glass of sherry and cured ham. There's a restaurant upstairs (where you'll pay more).

If you want a drink or something to eat, another choice is **Salon Puerta del Sol** at number 16, a beautiful eatery with stone walls and ornate carved wood.

You'll pass Calle de la Cruz and then arrive at the Plaza de Canalejas. Turn right onto Calle de Principe. Head down Calle de Principe.

You'll soon run into our next sight, the **Plaza Santa Ana**. This pleasant square is located in one of Madrid's oldest neighborhoods. This is where many Madrileños congregate on weekend evenings. It's home to **Teatro Español**, the city's oldest theater dating back to 1745 (it's to your left). Across the square is the stately Hotel Reina Victoria (now renovated and home to a Hard Rock Hotel). There are great places to take a break here, especially **Cervecería Alemana** at number 6. One street off of the square (at the end of Calle de Principe) is **Casa Alberto** at 18 Calle de las Huertas. This *taberna* and restaurant has been open since 1827. You'll have great *tapas* or main courses at reasonable prices, and the staff is exceptionally friendly. These two eateries are included in the *Tapas* Walk in this book.

Take a left onto Calle de Prado. You'll pass Calle de Echegaray and Calle de Ventura de la Vega. Turn right at Calle de León and then make a left onto Calle de Cervantes (the first street on your left).

You'll pass the **Casa de Cervantes** at the corner of Calle de Cervantes and Calle de León. This is where Cervantes, the author of *Don Quixote de la Mancha*, died. It's on the right side of the street.

Continue along Calle de Cervantes. It will turn slightly to the left at Plaza de Jesus.

You'll soon find yourself at the beautiful fountain **Fuente de Neptuno** on the Plaza de Cánovas del Castillo. The fountain is named after the Roman god of the sea. Across the square is the **Museo Thyssen-Bornemisza** at 8 Paseo del Prado. It contains an interesting and eclectic collection, acquired by the

Spanish government in 1993, featuring works by Picasso, Velázquez, Goya, El Greco and Rembrandt. It also has a collection of contemporary works, including some by Pollock, Lichtenstein and Kandinsky. It's closed on Mondays.

Head to your right down the Paseo del Prado.

That massive museum you'll see on your left is the Museo del Prado, one of Europe's greatest museums, with 7,000 paintings by such notables as Velázquez, Goya, El Greco, Titian, Botticelli, Murillo and Rubens. *Paseo del Prado, Tel. 91/3302800, Open Tue-Sun 9am-8pm, Admission €6, under 18 free. Free Sun, Metro: Banco de España or Atocha, www.museoprado.es.* The Cáson del Buen Retiro in El Retiro park behind the museum houses more of the museum's collection.

You can visit the museum, or if you walk past the museum, you'll see the Jardin Botánico, Madrid's large botanical garden (open daily, €2). Behind the museum is El Retiro, a 350-acre park. It dates back to the 1630s, and is filled with statues, fountains, a lake, and lots of locals (and tourists) enjoying this vast green space in the midst of Madrid. Art is showcased in the Palacio de Cristal and the Palacio de Velázquez, 19th-century pavilions in the park. We'll end our walk here.

TAPAS WALK
Approximate distance a half-mile. See map on the next page.

The Spanish love *tapas*. They're small amounts of nearly any kind of food, usually served with a small glass of wine, beer or spirit. The time between lunch and dinner is usually when most Spaniards frequent *tapas* bars. You can have a *porción* (small sample) or a *ración* (a larger serving). Bars that serve wine, beer and snacks/appetizers (both hot and cold) are known as *tascas*. *Tapeo* is the act of bar-hopping in the early evening, eating *tapas* and drinking, before Spain's very late dinner hour.

Remember that this is meant to be a walk, not a stagger. Like the Madrileños, you should enjoy a leisurely evening. Take your time at each place. Sample something you've never had

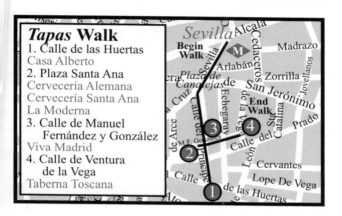

Tapas Walk
1. Calle de las Huertas
   Casa Alberto
2. Plaza Santa Ana
   Cervecería Alemana
   Cervecería Santa Ana
   La Moderna
3. Calle de Manuel
   Fernández y González
   Viva Madrid
4. Calle de Ventura
   de la Vega
   Taberna Toscana

before. You might discover that you actually like sardine heads.

A few tips that will help you with this walk: Many *tapas* bars don't take credit cards, and it's usually cheaper to order at the bar rather than at a table.

Our walk begins at the **Plaza Santa Ana**. *One way to reach the square is to take the metro to the Sevilla stop on Calle de Alcalá. Head south down Calle de Sevilla to the Plaza de Canalejas. Off of this plaza, head down Calle de Principe. You'll soon run into the Plaza Santa Ana but don't stop just yet. At the square (on your left) is the Teatro Español, the city's oldest theater dating back to 1745. If you continue past the square and keep walking, you'll run into Calle de las Huertas and our first stop.*

At number 18 is my favorite *tapas* bar in Madrid. Casa Alberto, a *taberna* and restaurant, has been open since 1827. You'll have great *tapas* or main courses at reasonable prices, and the staff is exceptionally friendly. Why don't you stand at the bar and have *albóndigas de ternera* (veal meatballs). They're fabulous! Down them with a glass of *vino tinto* (red wine).

Now head back to the Plaza Santa Ana.

This pleasant square is located in one of Madrid's oldest neighborhoods. This is where many Madrileños congregate on weekend evenings. In addition to the Teatro Español, the square is also home to the stately Hotel Reina Victoria, which has been renovated and is now the Hard Rock Hotel Madrid.

On the south side of the square are three places you can visit.

At number 6 is Cervecería Alemana, the best of the many *tapas* bars on the square, which was built in 1904 and modeled after a German beer hall (*Alemana* means "German" in Spanish). Have a beer. It'll be served in a white stein. Ernest Hemingway drank here, but that's really no big deal since he drank all over Madrid. Why don't you order *aceitunas* (olives), a popular snack? You'll be eating more later.

Another beer hall here is Cervecería Santa Ana at number 10. Here you can have a plate of *jamón y queso* (cured ham and cheese).

Another *tapas* spot here is La Moderna at number 12. Try a glass of delicious Spanish wine and a cheese plate, for which this place is known.

From the south side of the square, head across the square to the north side and turn right onto Calle de Manuel Fernández y González.

At number 7 is the popular bar Viva Madrid. It has fantastic tiled walls and an incredible carved ceiling. You come here to drink and, if you do stop, it's likely that the crowd will be young and lively.

Keep moving, eating and drinking! With Viva Madrid to your back, head left down Calle de Manuel Fernández y González. You'll pass Calle de Echegaray. The next street is Calle Ventura de la Vega. On the corner at 10-17 Calle de Manuel Fernández y González is our final stop.

At the tile bar Taberna Toscana, you'll sit on stools and taste a wide selection of *tapas* under sausages hanging from the ceiling. Try the fantastic *ternera* (veal) dish swimming in a delicious sauce (with french fries). A specialty here (if you're

Don't miss the indescribable (and unfinished) La Sagrada Familia by Antoni Gaudí, Barcelona's most recognizable landmark.

If you're the nosy type, you can visit some of the 3,000 rooms in the Palacio Real (Royal Palace) in Madrid.

I.M. Pei's glass pyramid at the Louvre in Paris, the greatest museum in the world.

The Eiffel Tower in Paris,
the most recognizable structure in the world.

The lovely and unspoiled village of Saignon in Provence.

Out for a night on the town? Whatever you want,
you'll probably find it in tolerant Amsterdam.

Amsterdam has more canals than Venice,
and more bridges than Paris.

The Brandenburg Gate in Berlin, a symbol of united Germany.

The Grand Canal, Venice's "main street."

St. Mark's Basilica on the Piazza San Marco in Venice.

The magnificent Trevi Fountain in Rome.

The immense Duomo in Florence.

The legendary city of London at night.

up to it) is *morcilla* (blood sausage). Try it. It's an interesting choice. When in Spain…

To return to where you began your walk, head back to the Plaza Santa Ana and then back up Calle de Principe to Calle Sevilla and Sevilla metro stop.

Convento de las Descalzas Reales
3 Plaza de las Descalzas Reales
Tel. 91/4548800
Open Sat and Tue-Thu 10:30am-12:30pm and 4pm-5:30pm,
Fri 10:30am-12:30pm, Sun 11am-1:30pm
Admission: €5. Guided tour only (45 minutes, in Spanish)
Metro: Puerta del Sol
www.patrimonionacional.es

Noblewomen who entered this convent in the mid-16th century brought incredibly rich dowries. Inside you'll find an incredible collection of tapestries, a chapel with an ornate gold altar, extraordinary statues, a piece of wood said to be from Christ's cross, and paintings by the likes of Titian and Goya.

Museo National Centro de Arte Reina Sofía
52 Calle de Santa Isabel
Tel. 91/4675062
Open Mon-Sat 10am-9pm, Sun 10am-2:30pm
Admission: €3. Free Sat after 2:30pm and Sun; under 18 and over 65 free
Metro: Atocha
www.museoreinasofia.es

If you travel to Madrid to see traditional art, you head for the Prado. If you're interested in 20th-century

Shopping Tip

EL CORTE INGLÉS
1-4 Calle de Preciados (and branches throughout the city)
Tel. 91/3798000
Open Mon-Sat 10am-9:30pm and some Sun
Metro: Puerta del Sol
www.elcorteingles.es
This is *the* department store in Madrid and all of Spain. Check out the supermarket on the lower level.

art, come here. This contemporary-art museum is housed in an 18th-century building that once was a hospital. There is an emphasis on 20th-century Spanish artists such as Picasso, Miró and Dalí. It's most famous painting is Picasso's masterpiece, *Guernica*, an anti-war painting of the bombing of the town of Guernica by the Germans during the Spanish Civil War. The museum recently opened a spectacular new wing, and there are great views from the transparent exterior elevators.

Restaurant Tips

CASA PACO
11 Plaza de Puerta Cerrada
Tel. 91/3663166
Closed Sun and Aug
Reservations required
Metro: La Latina

After a shot of red wine at the zinc-topped bar, you order steaks by weight in the tiled dining rooms. Grilled lamb and fish are also served. Moderate – Expensive.

EL BOGAVANTE DE ALMIRANTE
11 Calle de Almirante
Tel. 91/5321850
Closed Sun (dinner) and part of Aug

This restaurant and bar (the Boga Bar) has an attractive deep red-and-black décor. It's located in a cavelike basement with a brick vaulted ceiling. The food matches the setting and emphasizes seafood. If you're not in the mood for seafood, try the delicious *pato* (duck). Moderate – Expensive.

OMERTÀ
17 Calle de Gravína
Tel. 91/7010242
Open daily

This attractive restaurant and bar with brick-and-stone walls serves delicious pasta dishes and pizza. Try the penne with gorgonzola. Moderate.

Chueca
Neighborhood bounded on the south by the Gran Vía, on the west by Calle de Fuencarral, and on the east by the Paseo de Recoletas
Metro: Chueca

This trendy area is home to many cafés, shops and restaurants. A seat at a café on the Plaza de Chueca is one of the best places in Madrid to people-watch. Take a look at the beautifully decorated 1897 bar Bodega de Ángel Sierra on the square. It's the one with the fun and diverse crowd spilling onto the square.

Plaza de Toros de las Ventas
237 Calle de Alcalá
Tel. 91/7263570
Open: Sun Mar-Oct. Box office open Fri-Sun 10am-2pm and 5pm-8pm
Admission: Begins at €11
Metro: Ventas

It's certainly not for everyone, but attending a bullfight (*corrida*) is the quintessential Spanish experience. The free Museo Taurino (Bullfighting Museum) is also here.

Real Ermita de San Antonio de la Florida
Glorieta de San Antonio de la Florida
Tel. 91/5420722
Open Tue-Fri 10am-2pm and 4pm-8pm, Sat-Sun 10am-2pm
Admission: Free
Metro: Príncipe Pío (about a 10-minute walk from the metro stop along Paseo de la Florida)
www.munimadrid.es

Goya's "Sistine Chapel." Francisco de Goya painted the dome and vaults of this neo-Classical hermitage in 1798. After an extensive restoration, you can view this fantastic work featuring St. Anthony of Padua raising a man from the dead. Goya is buried here but not his head, which is said to have been taken by scientists who wanted to study his brain.

Museo de América
(Museum of the Americas)
6 Avenida de los Reyes Católicos (at Avenida Arco de la Victoria

Restaurant Tip

CASA MINGO
*34 Paseo de la Florida (across
the street from Goya's tomb)
Tel. 91/5477918
Open daily 11am-midnight
Metro: Príncipe Pío (about a
10-minute walk from the
metro stop)
No reservations. No credit
cards.*
You'll share sausages, roast
chicken and salad at long
tables with other diners at this
bodega (tavern). Cider (*sidra*)
is the drink of choice here.
Not to be missed! Inexpensive.

*next to the Faro de Madrid)
Tel. 91/5439437
Open Tue-Sat 9:30am-3pm,
Sun 10am-3pm
Admission: €3. Free Sun
Metro: Moncloa
www.museodeamerica.mcu.es*

Europe's best collection of
pre-Columbian, Spanish-
American, and Native
American artifacts is found
here. A few highlights are
the strangest collections:
shrunken heads, and
sculptures of people with
physical defects.

MADRID GETTING THERE/GETTING AROUND

Flights arrive at Barajas International Airport. There's a
tourist information center at the airport. The metro connects
with the airport (Aeropuerto/Barajas stop in Terminal 2). It's
a long (indoor) walk from the terminal to the metro stop.

Madrid's **metro** system is the easiest way to get around. Prices
are €1.30 for a single trip or €5.80 for 10 trips (more than one
person can use the ticket). They're also valid on the bus system
(except the bus to and from the airport). The metro operates
between 6am and 1:30am. **Buses** run between the airport and
Plaza de Colón every 10-15 minutes between 5am and 1:30am.
The trip costs €3 and takes between 45 minutes to an hour. A
taxi from the airport to central Madrid costs around €25.

Madrid's two **train** stations, Chamartín and Atocha, are both
on metro lines with access to the city center. Both train
stations have tourist information centers. The main bus
station is the Estacíon Sur, south of the city center. There are
also helpful tourist information centers at Plaza Mayor, 2

Calle de Duque de Medínaceli (near the Prado Museum), and the Atocha and Chamartín train stations.

PARIS

Paris is the most fabulous city in the world, not because of the Eiffel Tower or the Champs-Élysées, but because there's simply no other place in the world like it. It's called the City of Light, but perhaps it should be called the City of Promise. Around every corner is the promise of another beautiful street, another bistro filled with people eating delicious food (Paris is a city where you have to work at having a bad meal), another building that in any other city would be remarkable, but in Paris is just another building. Walk down practically any block in Paris, and the sights, smells and sounds will excite you.

Jardin des Tuileries
1st/Métro Tuileries or Concorde
West of the Louvre to the place de la Concorde

The same man who planned the gardens of Versailles designed the Tuileries. The garden takes its name from the word *tuil* or tile (roof-tile factories once were here). You'll enjoy bubbling fountains, statues, flowers and trees between the Louvre and place de la Concorde. Sit down and relax in this beautiful garden in the middle of Paris. Between the Tuileries and the Louvre is the Arc du Carrousel, a small triumphal arch, topped with four bronze horses.

Musée National du Louvre
1st/Métro Palais-Royal
34-36 quai du Louvre
Tel. 01/40.20.53.17 (recorded message)
Open Mon, Thu, Sat-Sun 9am-6pm; Wed and Fri 9am-9:45pm. Closed Tue

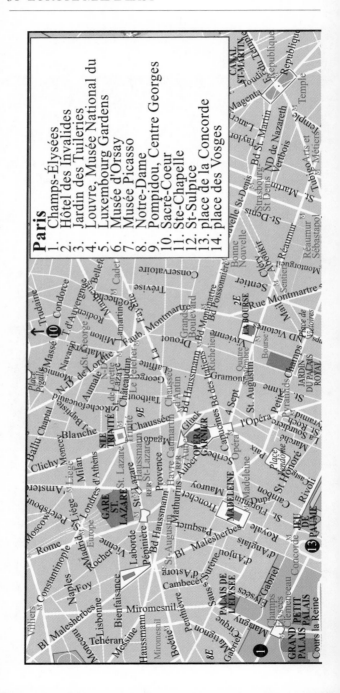

Paris
1. Champs-Élysées
2. Hôtel des Invalides
3. Jardin des Tuileries
4. Louvre, Musée National du
5. Luxembourg Gardens
6. Musée d'Orsay
7. Musée Picasso
8. Notre-Dame
9. Pompidou, Centre Georges
10. Sacré-Coeur
11. Ste-Chapelle
12. St-Sulpice
13. place de la Concorde
14. place des Vosges

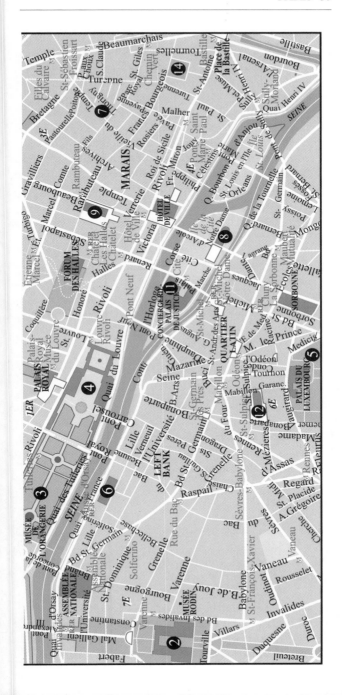

Admission: €8.50 (€6 after 6pm on Wed and Fri). Under 18 free and free the first Sunday of the month. €8.50 for exhibitions in Napoléon Hall. Combined permanent collection and temporary exhibits €13. Entry at 99 Carrousel du Louvre is quicker. www.louvre.fr

The Louvre is the greatest art museum in the world. With that said, if you have only a short stay in Paris, don't try to conquer the crowded museum at the expense of seeing the rest of Paris. It's the largest art museum in the world, the largest building in Paris, and it's in the largest palace in Europe.

The buildings that house the Louvre were constructed in the 13th century as a fortress. Today, the inner courtyard is the site of the controversial (but I think fantastic) glass pyramid designed by the famous architect I.M. Pei, that serves as the main entrance to the museum.

You'll find the following famous artworks (among the 30,000 here) at the Louvre:
• Leonardo da Vinci's *La Gioconda* (the *Mona Lisa*), *Virgin and Child with Saint Anne* and *Virgin of the Rocks*
• Michelangelo's *Esclaves* (*Slaves*)
• Titian's *Open Air Concert*
• Not to mention the *Venus de Milo*, *Winged Victory* ...

It really doesn't matter what you see and what you don't see. Just the experience of viewing so much famous art in one place is alone worth the trip to Paris.

Ste-Chapelle
1st/Métro Cité
4 boulevard du Palais
Tel. 01/53.40.60.80
Open daily Mar-Oct 9am-6pm, Nov-Feb 9am-5pm
Admission: €7 adults, €4 ages 18-25, under 18 free

On a sunny day, you'll be dazzled by nearly 6,600 square feet of stained glass at this Gothic masterpiece. The stained-glass windows owe their vibrant colors to the use of precious minerals and metals (gold for the red, cobalt for the blue).

Fifteen windows depict biblical scenes from the Garden of Eden to the Apocalypse (the large rose window). The chapel was built in 1246 to house what some believe to be the Crown of Thorns, a nail from the crucifixion and other relics.

Cathédrale Notre-Dame
4th/Métro Cité
6 place du Parvis Notre-Dame
Tel. 01/42.34.56.10
Open daily 7:45am-6:45pm. Tower open daily Apr-Oct 9:30am-7pm, Nov-Mar 10am-5:30pm
Admission: Free to the cathedral. Towers: €6, under 18 free.
Treasury: €3

Before construction of Notre-Dame began in 1163, the site was the home of a Roman temple to Jupiter, a Christian basilica, and a Romanesque church. Notre-Dame is one of the greatest achievements of Gothic architecture. Construction took nearly 200 years, and it has had a tumultuous history. Many treasures were destroyed during the French Revolution. At one point, it was even used as a food warehouse. The cathedral is so huge that it can accommodate over 6,000 visitors. The interior is dominated by three beautiful (and

Get the Museum Pass!

If art is your passion but you don't want to wait in lines to see it, you can purchase a Paris Museum Pass and have access to over 60 museums and monuments, including the Louvre and Musée d'Orsay. The cost is €30 for two consecutive days, €45 for four days, and €60 for six days. They're available at participating museums and many métro and bus stations.

huge) rose windows, and has a 7,800-pipe organ. Inside along the walls are individual chapels dedicated to saints. The most famous chapel is that of Joan of Arc in the right transept. The sacristy houses relics, manuscripts and religious garments. Note: free organ recitals take place most Sunday afternoons.

Restaurant Tip

LA FONTAINE DE MARS
7th/Métro École-Militaire
129 rue St-Dominique
Tel. 01/47.05.46.44
Red-checked tablecloths, friendly service and reasonable prices near the Eiffel Tower. When available, try the *poulet fermier aux morilles* (free-range chicken with morel mushrooms). Moderate.

Hôtel des Invalides
7th/Métro Invalides or La Tour-Maubourg
129 rue de Grenelle
Tel. 01/44.42.38.77
Open daily Oct-Mar 10am-5pm, Apr-Sep 10am-6pm. Closed first Mon of each month
Admission: €8, under 18 free

Built in 1670 for disabled soldiers, Les Invalides with its golden dome dominates the area around it. The world's greatest military museum, Musée de l'Armée (Army Museum), is here (everything from battles of the 1700s through World War II), as is the second tallest monument in Paris, the Eglise du Dôme (Dome Church). The main attraction here is Napoleon's Tomb, an enormous red stone sarcophagus. For such a tiny man, everything here is huge.

Musée d'Orsay
7th/Métro Solférino
1 rue de la Légion d'Honneur
Tel. 01/40.49.48.14
Open Tue-Sat 10am-6pm (Thu until 9:45pm), Sun 9am-6pm. Open at 9am from Jun 21 to Sep 18. Closed Mon
Admission: €7.50, €5.50 ages 18-25, under 18 free. €5.50 on Sun and after 4:15pm (after 8pm on Thu). Additional €1.50 for special exhibits

This glass-roofed museum is located across the Seine from the Tuileries and the Louvre in a former train station that has been gloriously converted into 80 galleries. Many of the most famous Impressionist and Post-Impressionist works are here, in a building that's a work of art in itself. There are works by Whistler, Manet, Degas, Renoir, Sargent, Pissaro and van Gogh, just to name a few. A magnificent museum, and so much more manageable than the Louvre.

The Restaurant du Musée d'Orsay serves a reasonably priced buffet lunch in an ornate dining room. Not bad for a museum restaurant.

Centre Georges Pompidou
4th/Métro Rambuteau
place Georges-Pompidou (on rue St-Martin between rue Rambuteau and rue St-Merri)
Tel. 01/44.78.12.33
Open 11am-10pm. Closed Tue
Admission: To the Center: €10, €8 ages 13-25, under 13 free. To the exhibits: €9 or €7 (depending on the exhibit), €7, €5 ages 13-25, under 13 free. To the Modern Art Museum only: €7, €5 ages 18-25, under 18 free. Free on the first Sun of the month
www.cnac-gp.fr

Named after Georges Pompidou, president of France 1969-1974, this museum of 20th- and 21st-century art is a must-see. The building is a work of art in itself. Opened in 1977, the controversial building is "ekoskeletal" (the plumbing, elevators, and ducts all are exposed and brightly painted). The ducts are color coded: blue for air conditioning, green for water, yellow for electricity, and red for transportation. Parisians call this "Beaubourg" after the neighborhood in which it's located. The Musée National d'Art Moderne (The National Museum of Modern Art) has works by Picasso, Matisse, Kandinsky, Pollock, and many other favorite modern artists. There's a great view from the rooftop restaurant (Georges). The Stravinsky Fountain and its moving mobile sculptures and circus atmosphere are found just to the south of the museum. Check out the red pouty lips in the fountain!

Musée Picasso
3rd/Métro St-Sébastien or St-Paul

5 rue de Thorigny
Tel. 01/42.71.25.21
Open Apr-Sep 9:30am-6pm, Oct-Mar 9:30am-5:30pm. Closed
Tue
Admission: €7, €5 ages 18-25, under 18 free. Free the first Sun
of the month

Often crowded, this museum has the largest Picasso collection in the world (not to mention works by Renoir, Cézanne, Degas and Matisse). Although there are no "masterpieces" here, this is a fine collection from every period of Picasso's artistic life. The museum is in the beautifully restored Hôtel Salé, which was built in the mid-1600s.

Marais
Métro St-Paul

The Marais is comprised of roughly the 3rd and 4th arrondissements on the Right Bank. This area, with its small streets and beautiful squares, is filled with interesting shops. It's home to both a thriving Jewish community and a large gay community. It's considered the *cœur historique*, historic heart of Paris, and has retained some of the flavor of the French Renaissance. Don't miss the place des Vosges, simply the most beautiful square in Paris, in France, and probably all of Europe.

Eglise St-Sulpice
6th/Métro Mabillon
place St-Sulpice (between the boulevard St-Germain-des-Prés
and the Luxembourg Gardens)
Open daily
Admission: Free

Located on an attractive square with a lovely fountain (the Fontaine-des-Quatre Points), this church has one of the largest pipe organs in the world with over 6,700 pipes. You'll notice that one of the two bell towers was never completed. Inside are frescoes by Delacroix in the Chapel of the Angels (Chapelle des Anges), a statue of the Virgin and Child by Pigalle, and Servandoni's Chapel of the Madonna (Chapelle de la Madone). Set into the floor of the aisle of the north-south transept is a bronze line. On the two equinoxes and the winter solstice, the sun reflects onto a globe and obelisk and from there to a crucifix. The obelisk reads: "Two scientists with God's help." You may find fans of the wildly popular novel *The Da Vinci Code* looking around the church, where it was the scene of a brutal killing in that book.

After you visit the church, head to the nearby **Jardin du Luxembourg** (Luxembourg Gardens). These formal gardens are the heart of the Left Bank.

Basilique du Sacré-Coeur
(Sacred Heart Basilica)
18th/Métro Anvers or Abbesses
place Parvis-du-Sacré-Coeur
Open daily 6am-11pm.
Observation deck and crypt 9am-7pm (until 6pm in winter)
Admission: Free. To the observation deck in the dome (and to the crypt) is 5€

To avoid climbing the hundreds of steps to the Basilica, you can take the métro to Abbesses, then take the elevator and follow the signs to the funicular (cable car), which will take you up to the Basilica for the price of a métro ticket.

At the top of the hill (*butte*) in Montmartre is the Basilica of the Sacred Heart which wasn't completed until 1919. The Basilica is named for Christ's heart which some believe is in the crypt. You can't miss the Basilica with its white onion domes and Byzantine and Romanesque architecture. Inside you'll find gold mosaics, but the real treat is the view of Paris from the dome.

MAJOR SIGHTS WALK
See map on pages 46-47. Approximate distance: five miles (two miles to place de l'Alma and three miles to Arc de Triomphe). Highlights: **Tour Eiffel**, **Bateaux Mouches**, **Arc de Triomphe**, and **Champs-Élysées**.

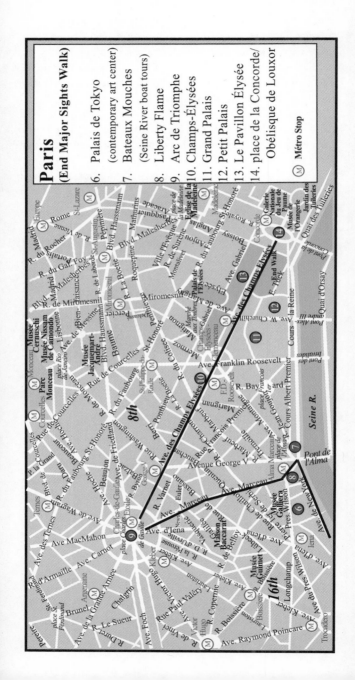

Paris
(End Major Sights Walk)

6. Palais de Tokyo
   (contemporary art center)
7. Bateaux Mouches
   (Seine River boat tours)
8. Liberty Flame
9. Arc de Triomphe
10. Champs-Élysées
11. Grand Palais
12. Petit Palais
13. Le Pavillon Élysée
14. place de la Concorde/
    Obélisque de Louxor

Ⓜ Métro Stop

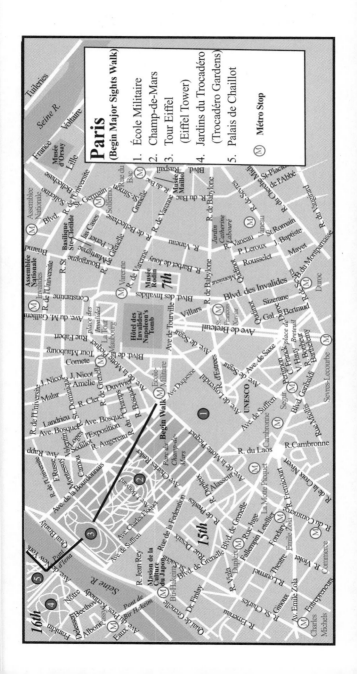

Paris
(Begin Major Sights Walk)

1. École Militaire
2. Champ-de-Mars
3. Tour Eiffel
   (Eiffel Tower)
4. Jardins du Trocadéro
   (Trocadéro Gardens)
5. Palais de Chaillot

Ⓜ Métro Stop

Take the métro to the Ecole Militaire stop.

At the métro stop, you'll see the huge **Ecole Militaire** (it's open only on special occasions). This Royal Military Academy was built in the mid-1700s to educate the sons of military officers. The building is a grand example of the French Classical style with its dome and Corinthian pillars. Its most famous alumnus is Napoleon.

Now start walking toward the Eiffel Tower.

The **Champ-de-Mars** are the long gardens that stretch from the Ecole Militaire to the Tour Eiffel (Eiffel Tower).

It's time to visit one of the best-known landmarks in the world. Visit the **Tour Eiffel** in either early morning or late evening when the crowds are smaller. It's without doubt the most recognizable structure in the world. You can either take the elevator to one of three landings, or climb the 1,652 stairs.

Walk behind the Eiffel Tower and cross the bridge (the Pont d'Iéna).

Once you cross the bridge, you'll be in the **Jardins du Trocadéro** (Trocadéro Gardens), home to the **Palais de Chaillot**. This huge palace, surrounded by more than 60 fountains, was built 60 years ago, and is home to several museums.

After taking in the gardens and palace, turn right (as you face the palace and gardens) on the avenue de New York along the Seine River.

While you're on the avenue de New York, you'll see the **Palais de Tokyo** on the left, a contemporary art center (and one of the most glamorous places for skateboarders).

Follow avenue de New York until you reach the Pont de l'Alma (the second bridge).

This bridge, the **Pont de l'Alma**, was created in the time of

Napoleon III. The original bridge was replaced in 1972 with the present-day steel structure. Take a look at one of the fanciest high-water markers in the world. Originally, there were four Second Empire soldier statues that decorated the old bridge. Only one, Zouave, remains below the bridge. Parisians use it to measure the height of the water in the Seine. In 1910, the water reached all the way to Zouave's chin.

You're now at the place de l'Alma, one of the most luxurious areas in Paris.

If you have never been in Paris (or for that matter, even if you have), you might want to take a tour of the Seine on the Bateaux Mouches. These boats depart from the Right Bank next to the place de l'Alma.

At the place de l'Alma, there's a replica of the torch of the Statue of Liberty.

The replica of the torch of the Statue of Liberty was erected here in 1987. It was meant to commemorate the French Resistance during World War II. It just happens to be over the tunnel where Princess Diana and her boyfriend Dodi Al-Fayedh were killed in an automobile crash in 1997. The Liberty Flame is now an unofficial shrine covered with notes, flowers and prayers to the dead princess.

If you've had enough walking, here's a good place to take the métro Alma Marceau back to your hotel. But if you want to continue, head down the avenue Marceau. It's one of the streets off of place de l'Alma. It's about a 10-minute walk on avenue Marceau to the Arc de Triomphe.

When you get to the Arc de Triomphe, don't try to walk across the square. This is Paris's busiest intersection. Twelve avenues pour into the circle around the Arc. There are underground passages, however, that take you to the monument. There's an observation deck providing one of the greatest views of Paris. There's no cost to visit the Arc, but there's an admission fee for the exhibit of photos of the Arc throughout history and for the observation deck. If you aren't impressed by the view down the Champs-Élysées, you really shouldn't have come to Paris.

Tired? If so, here's a good place to take the métro Charles-de-Gaulle-Étoile back to your hotel. But if you want to continue, head down the Champs-Élysées.

The left side of the Champs-Élysées has more interesting establishments than the banks and businesses on the right side. This street is home to expensive retail shops, fast-food chains, car dealers, banks, huge movie theatres and overpriced cafés. Despite this, you can sit at a café and experience great people-watching (mostly tourists).

On the left side, toward the end of the Champs-Élysées (at number 10) is Le Pavillon Élysée, an elegant oblong glass building built for the 1900 World's Fair. It's home to Lenôtre, a café, kitchen shop and cooking school all in one. Lenôtre's specialty is its desserts, and you can enjoy one with a cup of delicious coffee on the lovely stone terrace that looks onto the gardens.

Shopping Tip

One interesting shop is the large Sephora Perfume Store at 74 Champs-Élysées (open daily until midnight). The large "wheel of scents" lets you smell scents from chocolate to flower to wood!

At avenue Winston-Churchill you can gaze at the recently renovated Grande and Petit Palais, both built for the 1900 World Exhibition and, like the Eiffel Tower, never meant to be permanent structures. These magnificent buildings remain today in all their glory.

Continue down the Champs-Élysées until you reach the huge place de la Concorde.

At the end of your walk, admire the huge place de la Concorde. In the center of these 21 acres stands the Obélisque de Louxor (Obelisk of Luxor), an Egyptian column from the 13th century covered with hieroglyphics. It was moved here in 1833. Now a traffic roundabout, it was here that Louis XVI and Marie Antoinette were guillotined during the French Revolution.

You can take the Métro Concorde back to your hotel. The métro stop is at the far left side of the place de la Concorde.

The Concorde métro stop has 44,000 blue-and-white lettered ceramic tiles on its walls. Don't read French? I always wondered if they meant anything. In fact, they do. They spell out the seventeen articles of the declaration of the *Rights of Man and the Citizens* that the National Assembly adopted in 1789.

Restaurant Tips

LA MAISON
5th/Métro St-Michel
1 rue de la Bûcherie, Tel. 01/43.29.73.57
Open daily
An interesting crowd is found at this restaurant located near the Seine. In good weather, the tables on the small square in front of the restaurant make a great place to dine. Moderate.

LE TIMBRE
6th/Métro Notre-Dame-des-Champs
3 rue Ste-Beuve, Tel. 01/45.49.10.40
Closed Sat (lunch) and Sun
Good things come in small packages! The name means "stamp," appropriate for this tiny Left Bank bistro. The English chef serves interesting French dishes. Moderate.

PARIS GETTING THERE/GETTING AROUND
Paris has two international airports: Charles de Gaulle (Roissy) and Orly. At Charles de Gaulle, a free shuttle bus connects

Restaurant Tips

CHARTIER
9ʰ/Métro Grands Boulevards
7 rue du Faubourg-Montmartre, Tel. 01/47.70.86.29
No reservations

Traditional Paris soup kitchen with affordable prices. The *tripes à la mode de Caen* is a frequent special of the day (I passed on that). Lots of tourists, and you may be seated with strangers, but it's a great way to meet people. Inexpensive.

RESTAURANT DE LA TOUR
15ʰ/Métro Dupleix,
6 rue Desaix, Tel. 01/43.06.04.24
Closed Sun and Mon

You'll be welcomed by the friendly owners to the lovely dining room with Provençal décor where you'll dine on classic French fare. Try the delicious wild boar. After dinner, head to the brilliantly lit Eiffel Tower, just a few blocks away. Moderate.

Aérogare 1 with Aérogare 2. This bus also drops you off at the **Roissy train station.** Line B departs every 15 minutes from 5am to midnight to major métro stations. The cost is €8 (€13 for first-class). Connecting métro lines will take you to your final destination. The train stops at Gare du Nord, Châtelet-Les Halles, St-Michel and Luxembourg stations. The Roissy buses run every 15 minutes to and from the bus stop at Opéra Garnier on rue Scribe. (€8, about a one-hour trip). You can reach your final destination by taking the metro from the nearby Opéra metro station.

A taxi ride costs at least €40 to the city center. The price will be a bit higher than on the meter as a charge will be added for your baggage. At night, fares are up to 50% higher. You'll find the taxi line outside the terminals. It will frequently be long, but moves quite fast. Never take an unmetered taxi!

Minivan shuttles cost about €30 for two. One service is *www.parisairportservice.com, Tel. 01/55.98.10.80.*

Orly has two terminals: Sud (south) for international flights, and Ouest (west) for domestic flights. A free shuttle bus connects the two. A taxi from Orly to the city costs about €35 and up to 50% more at night. Orly Val is a monorail (stopping at both terminals) to the RER train station at Anthony (a ten-minute ride), then on to the city on the RER (Line B) train. The ride takes 30 minutes. The cost is €9 for both the monorail and the train ride.

Métro

The métro (subway) system is clearly the best way to get around Paris. It's orderly, inexpensive and for the most part safe. You're rarely far from a métro station in Paris. They are marked by a yellow **M** in a circle or by those incredibly beautiful Art Nouveau archways with "Métropolitain" on them. Although you may be confused when you first look at a métro map, simply follow the line that your stop is on and note the last stop (the last stop appears on all the signs) and you'll soon be scurrying about underground like a Parisian. Service starts at 5:30am. and ends between midnight and 1am. Métro tickets are also valid on the RER and buses. Each ticket costs €1.40. Buy a *carnet* (10 tickets for about €11).

PROVENCE

Some come to Provence for the savory cuisine and wonderful wines, while others visit to get away from it all in quiet villages. There are also some of the world's best-preserved Roman ruins to see, and elegant seaside resorts where you can bask on sun-drenched beaches. Color is the reason so many have fallen in love with the region, and why so many keep returning time after time. You'll be dazzled by fields of lavender, yellow sunflowers and bright red poppies under brilliant blue skies. Wherever you go, you'll create colorful memories.

Avignon
Population: 87,100
51 miles (82 km) northeast of Aix-en-Provence/60 miles (100 km) northwest of Marseille/425 miles (685 km) south of Paris

Avignon is located at the point where the Rhône and Durance rivers join. In 1309, when Pope Clément V arrived after fleeing the corruption of Rome, the town became the capital of Christendom for 68 years. Although the last pope left in 1377, you're reminded of the papal legacy everywhere in modern-day Avignon. Its large student population makes it a vibrant city unlike most of the small villages of Provence. The students, upscale boutiques and crowded cafés all make Avignon the most cosmopolitan city in Provence.

We'll take you on walks in the most visited cities in Provence: Avignon, Aix-en-Provence, and Arles. We'll also introduce you to other wonderful towns in Provence.

AVIGNON WALK

Our walk begins near the train station at the Porte de la République, one of the entries through the massive walls built by the Church. You'll be on cours Jean-Jaurés. Head down the right side of this street to the tourist office at 41 cours Jean-Jaurés. Here you can pick up a map of the city. Turn right out of the tourist office.

The street turns into rue de la République. This is the main street of Avignon and is filled with shops. At the corner of rue de la République and rue Frédéric Mistral at number 27 is our first stop.

Musée Lapidaire (closed Tuesdays), located in a Jesuit chapel, is filled with a collection of sculpture and stonework from the 1st and 2nd centuries.

Turn right at rue Frédéric Mistral, at the end of the street you'll run into another fine museum.

La Fondation Angladon-Dubrujead, at 5 rue Laboureur, is filled with the works of Picasso, van Gogh, Degas, Modigliani and Cézanne, to name a few. There's also a collection of furniture and art objects. Closed Mondays.

Continue down rue de la République and you'll find yourself at our next stop.

Place de l'Horloge is the heart of the city, filled with bistros, cafés, and restaurants. It gets its name from the Gothic clock tower (**Tour du Jacquemart**). Great people-watching! On the left is the **City Hall** (Hôtel de Ville) and a little further down on the left is the 19th-century **Opéra House**.

Off the place de l'Horloge is the place du Palais (rue Phillipe connects the two places). You make a right from place de l'Horloge at the Hôtel du Palais des Papes.

At the place du Palais, you'll find the Palais des Papes (the colossal Papal Palace to your right), the Petit Palais (straight ahead, the former residence of cardinals and bishops, and home of a museum devoted mostly to Italian paintings and sculptures from Avignon's churches), and the Cathédrale Notre-Dame des Doms (also to your right, with the tombs of two popes who ruled from Avignon. It's topped by the gold statue of the Virgin Mary). Visit the cathedral last.

With the cathedral to your back head right through the gates into our next sight.

Enter the promenade, and you'll head up into the Rocher-des-Doms (Rock of the Domes). You can enjoy the views across the Rhône River from this rocky bluff and garden. Huge pine trees, statues and swans make this a great place to relax. There's a small vineyard down the slope. From here, you can also look down at the four remaining arches of the Pont St-Bénézet (St. Bénézet Bridge) and the ruins in Villenueve-lès-Avignon across the river.

You can retrace your steps back to the rue de la République to return to the beginning of this walk.

Wine Tasting

You're in the heart of wine country. Look for signs saying *Cave Coopérative* at vineyards. If they say *dégustation*, this means that the winery offers free wine tastings. Although there's no obligation to buy, you should get at least one bottle (especially if you've spent some time at the winery).

Aix-en-Provence
Population: 139,000
19 miles (31 km) northeast of
Marseille/51 miles (82 km)
southeast of Avignon/110 miles
(176 km) west of Nice/474 miles
(760 km) south of Paris

Aix is a graceful and sophisticated city. Between the 12th and 15th centuries it was the capital of Provence. The Romans called it "Aquae Sextius" (Waters of Sextius) after the thermal springs that flow here and the Roman general (Caius Sextius Calvinus) who founded the city. Shaded squares with bubbling fountains in the Old Quarter, 17th-century town houses and the cours Mirabeau (the grand main avenue) make Aix a must for all visitors to Provence. It's a cultural center enhanced by thousands of students who attend one of France's oldest universities. The artist Paul Cézanne is from here, and created many of his best-known works here.

AIX-EN-PROVENCE WALK

Our walk begins at the tourist office at place Général-de-Gaulle at the Rotonde traffic circle. You can pick up a map here at the tourist office.

The black and white marble fountain at place Général-de-Gaulle (in the middle of the traffic circle) dates back to the 19th century, and features the figures of Fine Art, Agriculture and Justice at the top.

Head down the right side of cours Mirabeau.

This broad street lined with plane trees and stone buildings was built in the 17th century. You'll pass elegant buildings, four fountains, and many cafés and shops. This is the heart of Aix.

Stop at the corner of cours Mirabeau and rue du 4 Septembre.

One of the grand mansions on this street, the impressive Hôtel Maurel de Pontèves (now the Tribunal of Commerce) with its sculpted figures is at number 38 (on the corner).

In the middle of the cours Mirabeau is the Fontaine Moussue (it means "Mossy Fountain," and you'll understand why when you look at it).

Turn right onto rue du 4 Septembre.

You're now entering the Quartier Mazarin. It was here where Aix nobility built elegant town houses in the 17th and 18th centuries. After a short walk, you'll be at place des Quatre Dauphins dominated by its Baroque fountain.

Turn left onto rue Cardinale.

At place St-Jean-de-Malte on rue Cardinale (right before the church) you can stop in at the Musée Granet/Musée des Beaux-Arts (Closed Tues.) on the right side of the street. Located in a former priory, it's home to a collection of European art from the 16th to 19th centuries. You'll find eight Cézanne paintings here, along with a collection of his drawings and watercolors.

Next to the museum is one of Aix's many churches.

Drop in for a quick view of Eglise St-Jean-de-Malta. This Gothic church and chapel of the Knights of Malta (a charitable organization) is home to the tombs of the counts of Provence.

Make a left at rue d'Italie. Cross Place Forbin and the street turns into rue Thiers.

You're now in the Old Town, with its maze of streets and shops.

At the end of rue Thiers is place Verdun and place des Prêcheurs.

If you're taking this walk on Tuesday, Thursday or Saturday mornings, you'll run into a huge market at place Verdun where you can buy anything from antiques to clothes.

Circle around both places.

To your left is the Palais de Justice. In the center is an obelisk and to your right is the church Eglise de la Madeleine.

Turn around (heading back in the direction you entered the places), and find passage Agard.

Passage Agard (it has the words "Agard" written above it) is a covered passageway lined with shops.

Go through the passage and when you exit, you'll be back on the cours Mirabeau.

To your right as you exit the passage (at 53 cours Mirabeau) you can stop for coffee or a light snack at one of the sidewalk tables at Brasserie Les Deux Garçons. This 19th-century brasserie has been a meeting place for intellectuals and writers for years. Today, you'll also find quite a few tourists.

You can now head back down the cours Mirabeau to the beginning of our walk.

Arles
Population: 52,300
57 miles (92 km) northwest of Marseille/22 miles (36 km) south of Avignon/19 miles (31 km) southeast of Nîmes/450 miles (725 km) south of Paris

On the banks of the Rhône River, Arles is one of the three "A's" that make up the most visited cities in Provence (along with Aix-en-Provence and Avignon). Arles has everything you could want in a Provence city: festivals, an Old Town, Roman ruins, cafés (especially on la place du Forum) and intimate restaurants. Since Arles is situated at the head of the Rhône delta, it's on the route that linked Italy and Spain. When the Romans came into possession of Spain, Arles became an many important and strategic town for the Romans. Bullfights, still held in the arena, are a reminder of Arles's Spanish connection.

The folk culture and traditions of Arles are alive and well, and you'll see locals dressed in traditional Arlesian costumes on occasions. Van Gogh came here in 1888 and created some of his best-known paintings. Look around and you'll notice that many of the scenes featured in those paintings remain today.

ARLES WALK

We begin our walk at the tourist information center at the esplanade Charles de Gaulle on boulevard des Lices (part of the main road around the old town). Pick up a free map of the city here. As you exit the information center (with the center to your back), cross the street and head left down boulevard des Lices past the cafés. After rue Wilson watch for the stairs on your right (at Brasserie Lou Peyrou). Head up the stairs, down small rue Gageron to place Dr. Félix Rey.

Espace van Gogh is in the courtyard to your left and is open to the public (free admission). This is where Vincent van Gogh was sent after he cut off part of his left ear. The courtyard has been landscaped to match van Gogh's famous painting *Le Jardin de l'Hôtel-Dieu*.

With Espace van Gogh to your back, head left down rue President Wilson until you reach rue de la République. Number 29 is our next stop.

Women in traditional costumes greet you at the **Museon Arlaten** (Arles Museum), filled with regional clothes, furniture, portraits and art objects. The museum has a room dedicated to Frédéric Mistral, a poet from Provence who was awarded the 1904 Nobel Prize in Literature.

Continue down rue de la République (right as you're facing the museum) until you reach the large square.

The **place de la République** is the main square in Arles. Take in the **City Hall** (Hôtel de Ville) dating back to the 1600s. The **obelisk** with its carved features is thought to have been a trophy from the conquest of Egypt by Rome during the reign of Emperor Augustus.

On the place de la République is the town's main church, the **Eglise St-Trophime/Cloître St-Trophime**.

Admire the vivid frieze of the Last Judgment in the doorway, the 4th-century sarcophagus inside the church, and visit the cloisters, a masterpiece of medieval architecture. The left chapel holds relics of St-Trophime and other saints.

As you exit the church (with the church to your back), head right. Continue down pedestrian-only rue de l'Hôtel de Ville.

Turn right at rue des Arènes and head uphill. You'll soon find yourself facing our next stop.

You're now at one of the most spectacular Roman monuments in Provence. The well-preserved **Arena** (Arènes) with its two tiers of arches and four medieval towers once sat over 20,000

Detour

If you turn left down rue des Arènes, you'll run into la place du Forum. You can take a break at one of the many cafés, including Café de la Nuit. It's the one that looks like a vibrant van Gogh painting. Great people-watching here!

spectators. It still hosts bullfights. Great views of Arles from the top tier of the arena.

*Exit the arena (with the Arena to your back) and head left to visit the picturesque ruins of the **Théâtre Antique** (you'll cross place Bornier to rue de la Calade).*

Used today as a stage for festivals, this ancient theatre was built in the 1st century B.C. and seated 20,000. All that remains now are two columns.

Nîmes
Population: 137,200
26 miles (43 km) southwest of Avignon/19 miles (31 km) northwest of Arles

Officially part of the Languedoc region, Nîmes is a popular destination for visitors to Provence. Some of the world's best-preserved Roman sights are here, giving it the nickname "the Rome of France." The town is dotted with Roman ruins such as the Tour Magne (a tower on Mont Cavalier and the city's

Best Roman Sights in Provence

- **Pont du Gard** is a huge three-tiered, arched aqueduct spanning the Gardon River (13 miles southwest of Avignon)
- theatre and arena in Arles
- ruins and 2,000-year-old bridge (Pont Romain) in Vaison-la-Romaine
- Théâtre Antique and Arc de Triomphe in Orange
- ruins of a Gallo-Roman village (Glanum/Les Antiques) in St-Rémy
- Roman gate and tower in Nîmes

oldest monument). It's frenetic and not at all like the calm small villages of Provence. Did you know that denim (the material that all those jeans are made of) was created here in the Middle Ages? The Old Town is easily explored on foot and home to the major sights, including:

The steel-and-glass Carré d'Art (closed Mondays), a contemporary art museum.

The Maison Carrée is a Roman temple modeled after the Temple of Apollo in Rome.

The well-preserved arena (Amphithéâtre Romain) is a miniature of the Colosseum in Rome. Today, it's used for performances and an occasional bullfight.

Across the street from the arena is the Musée des Cultures Taurines (closed Mondays), a bullfighting museum.

The Musée Archéologique et d'Histoire Naturelle (closed Mondays), a museum of archaeology and natural history, is filled with statues, friezes, pottery, and coins.

The Cathédral Notre-Dame et St-Castor has a beautifully preserved Romanesque frieze featuring Adam, Eve, Abel, and Noah. The inside features a 4th-century sarcophagus.

Off of place aux Herbes (near the cathedral) is the Musée du Vieux-Nîmes (Museum of Old Nîmes) showcasing life in Nîmes in the Middles Ages, including a 14th-century jacket made of the famous *denim de Nîmes*, the fabric that Levi-Stauss used for blue jeans. The museum is closed on Mondays.

And don't miss the lively place de l'Horloge (Clock Square).

Lourmarin
Population 1,100
6 miles (10 km) south of Bonnieux

Lourmarin's winding narrow streets are lined with stone houses painted in shades of ochre and beige. It has a Renaissance chapel and both Catholic and Protestant churches. The village lies at the foot of the Luberon Mountain range which is covered with pine and oak trees. Surrounding the village are olive groves and vineyards. Although French vacationers discovered this little village years ago, it's now popular with foreign tourists. Its renovated *château* is the site of frequent concerts and exhibits.

Visitors have quite a few cafés and restaurants to choose from. It's become the gastronomic capital of the area. It's a lovely town with much to offer, and a great base for touring some of the prettiest towns of Provence.

Saignon
Population: 1,050
2 miles (3 km) southeast of Apt

Out of the way, but certainly worth the trip! This lovely, quiet, and unspoiled town high on a hill has picturesque shady squares, ancient fountains and ruins of ancient baths. The wood-carved doors of the Roman church Eglise Notre-Dame de Pitié depict Christ and Mary. The cemetery behind the church provides its permanent "residents" with a panoramic view of the countryside.

Oppède-le-Vieux
Population: 1,250
16 miles (26 km) southeast of Avignon/9 miles (14 km) south of Gordes

This hilltop village (don't confuse it with the lower modern town of Oppède), surrounded by thick forests, was deserted in 1900. The ruins of a medieval *château* loom above. In fact, much of the town itself is still in ruins, although some artists and writers have moved in and beautifully restored homes. You must park at the base of the hill (€2) and walk through a tiered garden filled with local plants labeled with their Latin, French and English names. Cross through the old city gate and walk up the steep alleys to visit the 13th-century church **Notre-Dame d'Alydon**, with its gargoyles and hexagon-shaped bell tower. Truly a taste of old Provence.

L'Isle-sur-la-Sorgue
Population: 17,200
16 miles (26 km) east of Avignon/25 miles (40 km) southeast of Orange

The name means "Island on the Sorgue River." I love this valley town. You'll find pedestrian bridges with flower boxes crossing graceful canals. The town is often referred to as the "Venice of Provence." Nine moss-covered waterwheels (that once powered the town's paper, silk and wool mills) remain along the canals. Only Paris is said to have more antique and secondhand shops in France. There are more than 300 shops

in this little town. Most are open daily. There's a huge antique fair at Easter. This otherwise quiet town is filled with crowds on Sunday. Stands loaded with local produce, crafts and antiques fill the streets along with street

performers. Browse the market and then watch others do the same at one of the many cafés. There's a more sedate market on Thursdays.

Uzès
Population: 8,000
15 miles (25 km) north of Nîmes/24 miles (39 km) west of Avignon

Don't bypass Uzès on the border of Provence in the Languedoc region. Begin your visit at the imposing Cathédrale St-Théodorit (you can't miss it and there's a large car park next to it). The cathedral, built on the site of a Roman temple, dates to 1652. Those are the remains of St-Firmin in the glass coffin on the left side of the cathedral. When outside, look up at the Tour Fénestrelle. Doesn't it look like the Leaning Tower of Pisa? As you face the cathedral, there's a former palace to your left that now houses the city's courts of law.

Across the street from the cathedral is the old town where you'll find the ducal palace on place du Duché. Descendents of the House of Uzès still live here (*Tel. 04/66.22.18.96, Open daily, admission: €10*). But don't come here just for the palace, come to walk the beautiful and car-free old town and to visit the medieval garden on rue Port Royal (*Open daily, admission: €2*). The place aux Herbes with sheltered walkways and medieval homes is a relaxing place to take a coffee break, although it's not so calm on Wednesday mornings and Saturdays when it hosts a lively market.

Cassis
Population: 8,000
19 miles (30 km) east of Marseille/25 miles (42 km) west of Toulon

Waterfront cafés around a beautiful port, buildings painted in pastel, boutiques and a medieval castle (the Château de Cassis) all make this Provence's most attractive coastal town. The water is clean and clear, and the beaches, like many others on this coast, are pebbly rather than sandy. The 1,200-foot cliff above the *château* is Cap Canaille, Europe's highest coastal cliff. Frankly, there isn't much to do in Cassis except lie on the beach and either look at the castle or the beachgoers, but, after all, that's what you came here for. Parking is scarce in town, so you can park outside and take a shuttle bus into town (watch for the signs saying "*navette*"). They're free and depart every 15 minutes.

PROVENCE GETTING THERE/GETTING AROUND
The Nice-Côte d'Azur Airport is located on a peninsula between Nice and Antibes. It's 20 minutes west of the central

city of Nice. The Marseille Airport (located in Marignane) is 17 miles northwest of the city. All major car rental companies are represented at both airports.

AMSTERDAM

Amsterdam has more canals than Venice, more bridges than Paris, more bicycles than cars, and perhaps more tolerance than any other city in the world. It's what makes Amsterdam truly unique ... and such a wonderful place to visit. It is easy to get around, and her sights are as diverse as its residents, including beautiful churches, lovely gardens, and, of course, the infamous Red-Light District. If you're interested in museums, there's something for everyone, from the famous Rijksmuseum offering paintings from the Dutch Golden Age to the Stedelijk Museum's contemporary art, and much more!

Canals
Amsterdam's canals and the Golden Age homes that line them make Amsterdam a unique destination. The tree-lined Brouwersgracht (Brewers Canal) is at the northern end of the Jordaan neighborhood. It offers incredibly beautiful views down the four main canals (Prinsengracht, Keizersgracht, Herengracht, and Singel).

Anne Frankhuis
(Anne Frank House)
263 Prinsengracht
Tel. 020/556-7100
Open daily 9am-7pm, closed Jewish holidays
Admission: €8, €4 ages 10-17, under 10 free
www.annefrank.nl

Anne Frank's hiding place, where she penned her famous diary, comes to life in this poignant museum.

Restaurant Tips

The Jordaan and northern part of the canal belt are home to many great restaurants. There is plenty of diverse cuisine to choose from (Dutch, Italian and Spanish, to name just a few) on Lindengracht alone. Here are two more:

SEASONS
16 Herenstraat
Tel. 020/330-3800
Open Wed-Sat noon-3pm and 6pm-10:30pm, Sun noon-4pm and 6pm-9:30pm
www.seasonsrestaurant.nl
Friendly restaurant serving international fare and excellent wines. Highly recommended! Moderate.

RESTAURANT DE BELHAMEL
60 Brouwersgracht
Tel. 020/622-1095
Open daily 6pm-10pm
This restaurant has a beautiful small bar and an excellent reputation. The view down the canal adds to the charm. Moderate – Expensive

Rijksmuseum
(Royal Museum)
1 Jan Luijkenstraat(along Stadhouderskade)
Open daily 9am-6pm
Tel. 020/674-7000 or 670-7047
Admission: €9, under 19 free
www.rijksmuseum.nl
Trams: 2 and 5 (to Hobbemastraat)

The Royal Museum is one of the world's greatest art museums with masterpieces by Rembrandt, Vermeer, and countless others.

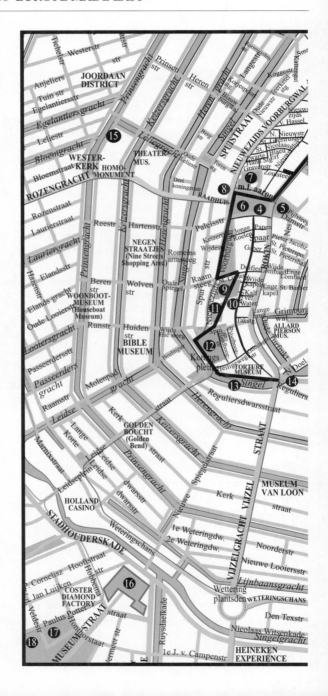

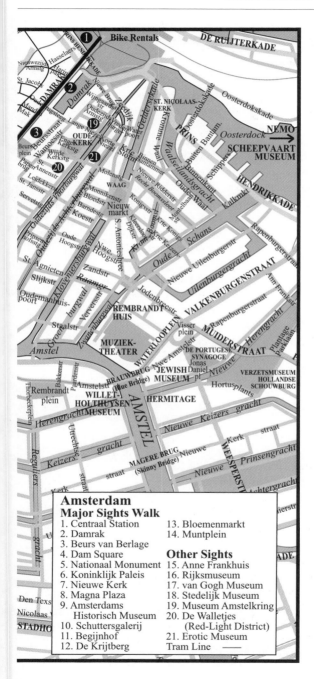

Amsterdam
Major Sights Walk
1. Centraal Station
2. Damrak
3. Beurs van Berlage
4. Dam Square
5. Nationaal Monument
6. Koninklijk Paleis
7. Nieuwe Kerk
8. Magna Plaza
9. Amsterdams
   Historisch Museum
10. Schuttersgalerij
11. Begijnhof
12. De Krijtberg
13. Bloemenmarkt
14. Muntplein

Other Sights
15. Anne Frankhuis
16. Rijksmuseum
17. van Gogh Museum
18. Stedelijk Museum
19. Museum Amstelkring
20. De Walletjes
    (Red-Light District)
21. Erotic Museum
Tram Line ——

van Gogh Museum
7 Paulus Potterstraat
Tel. 020/570-0200
Open daily 10am-6pm (Fri until 10pm)
Admission: €10, €3 ages 13-17, under 13 free
www.vangoghmuseum.nl

More than 200 paintings, nearly 600 drawings and sketches, and hundreds of van Gogh's letters are found here. From his early 1880s paintings to the works of his later years of torment, these works demonstrate not only the development of van Gogh's art, but also of his fascinating life. In addition to van Gogh's art, the works of such notables as Gauguin, Toulouse-Lautrec, Bernard, and Monet are also on display here, along with some of van Gogh's extensive collection of Japanese drawings.

Stedelijk Museum of Modern Art
13 Paulus Potterstraat (closed for renovation)
Currently located in a temporary space in the Eastern Docks area
at 5 Oosterdokskade near Centraal Station
Tel. 020/573-2911/020/573-2737 (information)
Open daily 10am-6pm (Thu until 9pm)
Admission: €9
www.stedelijkmuseum.nl
(in Dutch)

This museum, one of the world's most prestigious modern-art museums, is housed in a neo-Renaissance building constructed in 1895. You'll find works by Manet, Monet, Picasso, Pollock, Warhol, Chagall, and Cézanne, and pieces by many Dutch artists such as Appel and Mondrain. From paintings to video to photography, there is an impressive display of contemporary works here.

Restaurant Tip

ZUID ZEELAND
413 Herengracht
Tel. 020/624-3154
Open Mon-Fri noon-2:30pm
for lunch, daily 6pm-11pm
for dinner
www.zuidzeeland.nl
This bustling restaurant with contemporary décor serves straightforward international fare. Its menu features a delicious and interesting deer tenderloin, and an extensive wine list. Expensive.

De Walletjes/De Wallen
(Red-Light District)
Behind Dam Square between
Oudezijds Voorburgwal and
Oudezijds Achterburgwal
www.red-light-district.nl

The oldest profession in the world sells itself (legally) in a new type of window-shopping. From sex clubs to live sex shows, sex is a big part of Amsterdam's tourist industry. Locals don't bat an eye at any of this, but you might. If you're not interested in seeing any of it, stay away from the Red-Light District and the area around it. You can easily visit Amsterdam's other wonderful sights without encountering any of the sex industry.

Coffeeshops?

What's that smell? It certainly isn't coffee. Because of Amsterdam's tolerant attitude to certain drugs, you'll find them "served" in the city's numerous coffeeshops.

Museum Amstelkring
(Our Dear Lord in the Attic Museum)
40 Oudezijds Voorburgwal at Heintje Hoekssteeg (on the edge of the Red-Light District)
Tel. 020/624-6604
Open Mon-Sat 10am-5pm, Sun 11am-5pm
Admission: €6
www.museumamstelkring.nl

After the Protestant Reformation, Catholics were forced to worship secretly in clandestine churches. In the mid-1660s, three canal houses were purchased for the purpose of housing a "secret" church. The highlight is in the attic where you'll be shocked to find a beautiful church complete with pews that can seat 150 people, an 18th-century organ, and an ornate Baroque altar.

Erotic Museum
54 Oudezijds Achterburgwal
Tel. 020/624-7303
Open Thu-Mon 11am-1am (Fri-Sat until 2am)
Admission: €4

It's appropriate that the Erotic Museum is located in the Red-

Light District. The history of S&M, porn, sex shows–you get the idea–are on display at this museum. Lots of mannequins doing naughty things. It proudly displays erotic drawings by John Lennon.

Gay Amsterdam
www.gayamsterdam.com (information)

Gays and lesbians have long had equal rights in the Netherlands, and same-sex marriage has been legal here since 2001. The city is a huge destination for gay and lesbian travelers, especially during Gay Pride Parade held the first week in August. The Homomonument (Homosexual Monument), next to the Westerkerk Church, is the first of its kind in the world. It's dedicated to homosexuals who were rounded up by the Nazis during World War II, forced to wear pink triangles, and sent to concentration camps. There are many gay hotels, bed and breakfasts, restaurants, and bars. Some bars around the city are listed below:

- April, 20 Reguliersdwarsstraat, *www.april-exit.com*
- Exit, 42 Reguliersdwarsstraat, *www.april-exit.com*
- Queen's Head, 20 Zeedijk, *www.queenshead.nl*
- Barderij, 14 Zeedijk

Bike Rentals
You may look on in horror at the thousands of bicyclists crisscrossing with speeding automobiles in Amsterdam. If you think you're up to it, try renting a bike. It can be great fun and an easy way to see a lot of the city. One company, Mac Bike, rents for a minimum of two hours, by the day, and longer. Daily rental prices begin at €7 for a standard bicycle with footbrake. The main location is next to Centraal Station at 12 Stationsplein, *Tel. 020/624-8391*. See Amsterdam as the locals do! *www.macbike.nl*

MAJOR SIGHTS WALK
Highlights: Dam Square, Begijnhof, and Flower Market. See Major Sights map on pages 68-69. Approximate length of walk: one mile.

Our walk begins at the Stationsplein, the bustling square in front *of **Centraal Station**. With Centraal Station to your back, cross the Open Haven Front (that's the body of water right in front of the Stationsplein). The street in front of you is Damrak.*

The first street that most travelers to Amsterdam explore is Damrak, the main street connecting Centraal Station and Dam Square. It's filled with fast-food outlets, and souvenir shops selling everything from wooden shoes to Dutch chocolate. It's probably Amsterdam's least attractive street.

*Head down Damrak. You'll pass the Sex Museum on your right and the huge **Beurs van Berlage** (the former stock exchange) on your left. It's now used as a convention center and is home to the Netherlands Philharmonic Orchestra. Soon you'll reach a large square. You can't miss it.*

You're now at Dam Square. The 70-foot white obelisk here is the Nationaal Monument (National Monument). It was built in 1956 as a war memorial dedicated to those who endured World War II and the Nazi occupation. The urns at the back of the monument contain earth from each Dutch province and its former colonies: Indonesia, The Netherlands Antilles in the Caribbean, and Suriname in South America.

Detour

Need a drink before you visit the major sights on this walk? Take a right off of Damrak onto Zoutsteeg. This little street is just before the De Bijenkorf, Amsterdam's best-known department store (on the left side of Damrak). At number 7 Zoutsteeg is Helen van Troye, the self-proclaimed smallest pub in Amsterdam. Have a drink at this friendly bar.

The massive Koninklijk Paleis (Royal Palace) was built in the mid-1600s (closed Mondays except in July and August). Originally it served as City Hall, became a royal residence under the rule of Napoleon, and a royal palace of the House of Orange. The royal family doesn't live here anymore.

Head for the public entrance of the Royal Palace.

The marble-floored **Burgerzaal** (Citizens Chamber) runs the length of the second floor of the palace. You'll find mighty Atlas holding a globe and maps in the floor portraying Amsterdam as the center of the world.

As you face the Royal Palace, head to your right to the large church.

The **Nieuwe Kerk** (New Church) dates back to the early 1400s. Check out its stark interior as this former Catholic church lost most of its decorations and statues during the Iconoclasm of 1566 (when the Protestants destroyed the icons, statues and other decorations of Catholic churches). It now houses changing exhibits.

Now head for a street with the long name of Nieuwezijds Voorburgwal (behind the Royal Palace and Dam Square). The opulent building at 182 used to be a post office. Now it's all about shopping.

The **Magna Plaza** was built in 1899 and now it houses over 40 stores on five stories. Go inside if you're in the mood to shop. Closed Sunday mornings.

Continue down Nieuwezijds Voorburgwal (to your right with the Magna Plaza to your back). Turn left onto Sint Luciënsteeg. At number 27 is one of three entrances to one of the best museums in Amsterdam, the Amsterdams Historisch Museum. Enter the courtyard. To your right is the museum entrance.

Before you enter the museum, notice the 47 wall plaques preserved from buildings throughout the city that were either demolished or renovated.

The **Amsterdams Historisch Museum** (Amsterdam Historical Museum), once a 17th-century orphanage, chronicles the history of Amsterdam from fishing village to modern metropolis. You'll find paintings (including Rembrandt's partly damaged and ghastly *Anatomy Lecture of Dr Jan Deijman*), maps, wearing apparel, jewelry, prints, porcelain, sculpture and archeological finds. *Tel. 020/523-1822. Open Mon-Fri 10am-5pm, Sat-Sun 11am-5pm. Admission: €6, €3 ages 6-16, under 6 free. www.ahm.nl.*

If you don't want to visit the museum (or if you have finished your visit to the museum), head to your left. In between the courtyard of the Amsterdam Historical Museum and the Begijnhof is our next sight.

The **Schuttersgalerij** (Civic Guards Gallery) is a glass-covered passageway filled with a group of huge early 1600s portraits of the city's civic guards who were initially responsible for the safety of the city, but later became fraternal groups.

At the end of the gallery, exit out onto Gedempte Begijnensloot. Walk a short while down this narrow alley until you see the entrance to the courtyard on your right side. Enter the courtyard.

The **Begijnhof** (Beguine Court) is open daily until sunset. The courtyard of this 14th-century *hofje* (almshouse) is a peaceful getaway from the bustling city. Founded in 1346 by members of a lay Catholic sisterhood (the Beguines), it's still the home of elderly poor women. There's a statue of a Beguine, dressed in traditional habit, in the center. You can see the **English Reformed Church** (Engelse Kerk) dating back to the late 1300s, and the **Mother Superior's House** (number 26). The **Begijnhof Chapel** opposite the English Reformed Church houses a clandestine church (like Our Dear Lord of the Attic above). *Courtyard: Open daily 9am-5pm (entry through the gateway at Gedempte Begijnensloot). Chapel: Open Mon 1pm-6:30pm, Tue-Fri 9-6:30pm, Sat-Sun 9am-6pm (entry to chapel after 5pm is through the gate off of Spui). Admission: Free. www.begijnhofamsterdam.nl*

Cornelia Arents was the mother superior of the Beguines and died in 1654. She was buried in the English Reformed Church against her wishes (she was a Roman Catholic and did not wish to be buried in a Protestant church). Arents is said to have announced that she would rather be buried in the gutter. According to legend, the morning after her burial, her coffin was found in the gutter next to the lawn outside the church. That's why you'll see a grave in the gutter. A wall plaque next to the lawn outside the church reads "Beguine Cornelia Arents was laid to rest in this gutter at her own request. May 2, 1654."

Look for number 34.

At number 34 in this courtyard is the **Het Houten Huis** (City's Oldest House). It dates back to about 1475.

After passing the oldest house, head through the arched doorway. Follow the stairs that lead to the square Spui.

The small **Spui** square is filled with bookshops, bars and cafés. **Café Hoppe**, a brown café (brown from all of the cigarette smoke that has darkened its walls) has been in business for over 300 years. The statue **Little Darling** (Het Lieverdje) here is of an urchin (the one with hands on hips). It's said to be a symbol of Amsterdam: Always full of life and a little mischievous. There's a book market here on Fridays and an art market on Sundays. A great place to stop at a café.

Take a right and walk straight to the pedestrian-only street Heisteeg. Continue over the bridge Heiburg and then take a left at Singel. Our next sight is at number 446.

You can't miss the two steeples of this 1880s neo-Gothic church. The name **De Krijtberg** means "chalk church" since the church was built on the site of a home owned by a chalk merchant. Its real name is **Franciscus Xaveriuskerk** (St. Francis Xavier Church). Head inside to take a look at the statue of St. Francis Xavier to the left of the altar, the detailed wood carving of the Immaculate Conception near the pulpit, and the statue of St. Ignatius, the founder of the Jesuits, to the right of the altar.

Continue down the Singel. Our next sight is between Koningsplein and Muntplein.

Stalls selling cut flowers and bulbs are sold from "floating" anchored barges on the Singel Canal. The **Bloemenmarkt** (Flower Market) (closed Sunday) is incredibly fragrant, and a great photo opportunity. If you buy bulbs to take back home, make sure they have a sticker on them saying that they're approved by Customs to bring into the country.

At the end of the Flower Market is Muntplein.

The Munttoren (Mint Tower) on the square Muntplein gets its name from the time when it was used as a mint during the French occupation of the city in the 1600s. Its bells ring every 15 minutes. You can end your walk at one of the cafés here.

AMSTERDAM GETTING THERE/GETTING AROUND

Schiphol Airport, only 8 miles (13 km) from central Amsterdam, is one of the busiest in the world. It's also one of the most convenient. To reach Centraal Station (the main train station in Amsterdam), trains depart from the airport train station (downstairs from Schiphol Plaza) every 15 minutes (hourly 1am-5am). Get on the train that says "Amsterdam CS." The one-way fare is less than €4. The trains are clearly marked, and there are kiosks with instructions in English. A taxi costs nearly €40 to central Amsterdam. Buses are slower, and depart from Schiphol Plaza. They aren't much cheaper than the train. There's a hotel shuttle bus (Connexxion) that operates from Schiphol Plaza that takes you to about 20 main hotels for around €9 (buy the ticket on the bus).

Trams are frequent and easy-to-use. Buses fill the gap between 1-6am. Amsterdam's Metro (subway) is used mostly for travel to the suburbs. You can buy a tram ticket (€1.60) from the driver or, on some trams, from a machine in the middle of it. You can buy a *strippenkaart* from the post office, rail and bus stations, or tobacco shops. Each trip is one strip. You stamp the ticket in the yellow machine on the tram. More than one person can use the card. You just stamp it for how ever many people are using it. Once stamped, the ticket is valid for one hour (including all transfers). An eight-strip card costs €5.60 and a 15-strip card costs €6.40. There are also day and week passes available. Stops are announced and posted as you approach.

BERLIN

Berlin is like no other city in the world. Despite the ravages of war, the brutal division of the wall and the struggles of reunification, Berlin continues to look forward. You can marvel at historic buildings painstakingly renovated (such as the impressive Reichstag), or experience some of the most innovative modern architecture anywhere (and, particularly at Alexanderplatz in former East Berlin, some of the worst). But Berlin isn't about buildings. It's about feeling alive and vibrant. There's something for everyone. From museums like the Pergamonmuseum, with some of the world's greatest masterpieces, to poignant memorials like the Memorial to the Murdered Jews, to an exciting nightlife unlike any other city in Europe, Berlin will not disappoint.

Reichstag
(Parliament Building)
Platz der Republik
Tel. 22732152
Open daily (entry through
metal detectors) from 8am-
midnight (you must enter before 10pm)
Admission: Free
S-Bahn: Unter den Linden
www.bundestag.de

The seat of the German Parliament tells the story of Germany and Berlin. This neo-Renaissance building was constructed between 1884 and 1894. The inscription on the front of the building says "Dem Deutschen Volke" ("To the German People"). Fire broke out here in 1933 and destroyed much of it. It's believed that followers of Hitler started it, but the Communists were blamed. This infamous event allowed Hitler to round up and arrest "enemies" of the government. Allied bombing heavily damaged it at the end of World War

II. You can still see graffiti carved by Soviet soldiers on the interior walls. Most of the ornamentation and the central dome were removed after the war during reconstruction, and the building was not used from 1933 to 1999. It sat forlornly near the Berlin Wall. In 1995, the artist Christo wrapped the entire building in fabric.

The building took on new meaning after reunification when Berlin was restored as the capital of Germany, and, since April 1999, the Reichstag is again the seat of the Bundestag (the German parliament). Today's design is by British architect Sir Norman Foster, who added a fantastic glass dome. The dome can be reached by taking the elevator. You then walk up spiral ramps to the top (there's also a rooftop restaurant). At night, the dome is lit from inside. The lobby features a huge 60-foot German flag. Modern buildings housing federal government offices flank the Reichstag.

Gendarmenmarkt
(Gendarmen Market)
U-Bahn: Französische Strasse

This beautiful square features three stunning buildings:
• Konzerthaus *(Concert House)*
• Französischer Dom *(French Cathedral)*
• Deutscher Dom *(German Cathedral)*

Museumsinsel
(Museum Island)
An island in the Spree River at the eastern end of Unter den Linden
S- and U-Bahn: Friedrichstrasse

Several museums (described below) are all found on this island in the Spree River.

Bodemuseum *(Bode Museum)*: This museum will ultimately

Restaurant Tip

BORCHARDT
47 Französische Strasse
Tel. 81886262
Open daily 11:30am-2am
U-Bahn: Französische Strasse
A French bistro in Berlin. Good food and friendly service are the reasons to visit this very popular, very attractive restaurant located near Gendarmenmarkt. Moderate-Expensive.

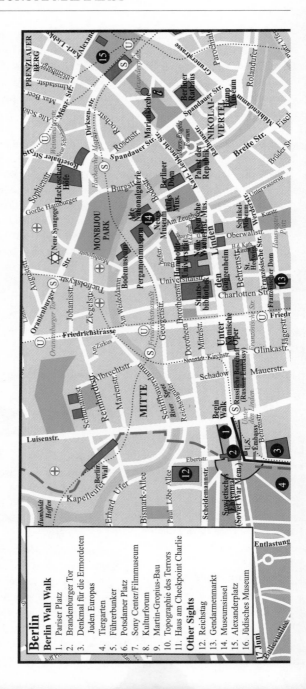

Berlin

Berlin Wall Walk
1. Pariser Platz
2. Brandenburger Tor
3. Denkmal für die Ermordeten Juden Europas
4. Tiergarten
5. Führerbunker
6. Potsdamer Platz
7. Sony Center/Filmmuseum
8. Kulturforum
9. Martin-Gropius-Bau
10. Topographie des Terrors
11. Haus am Checkpoint Charlie

Other Sights
12. Reichstag
13. Gendarmenmarkt
14. Museumsinsel
15. Alexanderplatz
16. Jüdisches Museum

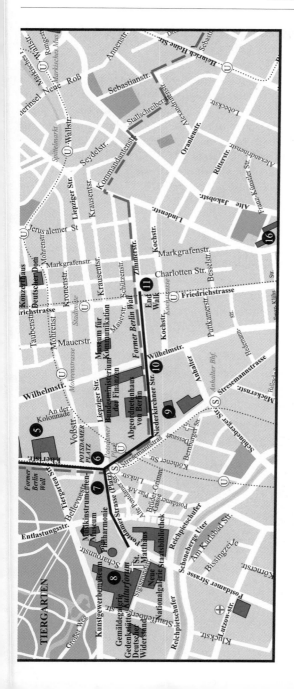

house the Museum of Byzantine Art, Collection of Antique Sculpture, and Coin Cabinet.

Altes Museum *(Old Museum)*: This museum contains a collection of Roman and Greek antiquities. The museum is now also the home of the Ägyptisches Museum (Egyptian Museum) dedicated to the art of ancient Egypt. The famous bust of Nefertiti (created over 3,000 years ago and discovered by German archeologists in 1912) will be a highlight of your visit. The Egyptian Museum will move to the Neues Museum (also on Museum Island) before 2010. *Tel. 2095055. Tue-Sun 10am-6pm. Admission: €8.*

Pergamonmuseum *(Pergamon Museum)*: Perhaps the best museum in Berlin. It's one of the world's largest museums of archeology. Highlights include the Pergamon Altar, a huge (and I do mean huge) altar dating back to 160 B.C. It also houses a museum of Islamic art and has a massive collection of antiquities from the Near East. *Tel. 20905577. Open Tue-Sun 10am-6pm (Thu until 10pm). Admission: €8.*

Berliner Dom *(Berlin Cathedral)*: This Italian Renaissance-style cathedral has been restored to its former, and ornate, glory. The views from the stupendous green copper dome are great. Hope you like to climb steps, as there are 270 of them. Its crypt

contains the remains of the House of Hohenzollern, the Prussian rulers from 1701-1918. Frequent concerts are held here featuring the cathedral's 7,000-pipe organ. *Tel. 202690. Open Mon-Sat 9am-7pm, Sun noon-7pm. Admission: €5.*

Alte Nationalgalerie *(Old National Gallery)*: Germany's largest collection of 18th-, 19th- and early 20th-century art and sculpture is housed in this impressive building. You'll find works by such notables as Rodin, Manet, van Gogh, Degas, Pissaro, Rodin, Monet, Cézanne and Berlin's own von Menzel.

Tel. 20905566. Open Tue-Sun 10am-6pm (Thu until 10pm). Admission: €8.

Neues Museum *(New Museum)*: This museum will house the Egyptian Museum and the Primeval and Early History Museum when it's completed before 2010.

Palast der Republik *(Palace of the Republic)*: Can you say 1970s? This unattractive monstrosity, abandoned since the 1990s, is the former home of the parliament of the old GDR (East Germany). There are endless debates about what to do with it. It's now scheduled for demolition and who knows if it will be standing by the time you get here.

Alexanderplatz
(Alexander Square)
Between Karl-Liebknecht-Strasse and Grunerstrasse
U- and S-Bahn: Alexanderplatz

The East German government developed this huge square in the 1960s and 1970s and you can tell! I visited here in the 1980s and it was a weird experience, as the square was then and continues to be both ugly and fascinating. Hideous communist-era buildings are dominated by a huge television tower (Fernsehturm). *Tel. 2423333. Open Nov-Feb 10am-midnight, Mar-Oct 9am-1am. Admission: €7.* The fountain here (the one with all the graffiti on it) has a wonderfully communist name: Brunnen der Völkerfreundschaft or "Fountain of the Friendship of Peoples." The silly-looking world clock (Weltzeituhr) with an atom design on top (you have to see it to understand) will tell you the time in such important communist strongholds as Havana and Hanoi.

Unter den Linden
The street running east to west from the Brandenburg Gate to Museumsinsel
S-Bahn: Unter den Linden

This famous street got its name from the thousands of linden trees that line it. In the 1920s, this was one of Europe's grandest boulevards. Although most of the buildings were destroyed in World War II, many have been restored. Today, it's vibrant and a great place to stroll.

Jüdisches Museum Berlin
(Jewish Museum Berlin)
9-14 Lindenstrasse
Tel. 25993300
Open Mon 10am to 10pm and Tue to Sun 10am to 8pm
Admission: €5
U-Bahn: Kochstrasse
www.jmberlin.de

The building housing this museum is itself worth the trip. Representing a shattered Star of David, the theme here is disorientation, emptiness and darkness. This museum tells

Restaurant Tips

The neighborhood of Prenzlauer Berg (northeast of the city center) is fast becoming a trendy area with many fine restaurants, including:

TRATTORIA PAPARAZZI
35 Husemannstrasse
Tel. 4407333
No credit cards
Open daily 6pm-1am
U-Bahn: Eberwalder Strasse

Popular *trattoria* serving hearty Italian fare at reasonable prices. Friendly service. Moderate.

GUGELHOF
37 Knaackstrasse
Tel. 4429229
Open Mon-Fri 4pm-1am, Sat and Sun 10am-1am
U-Bahn: Eberwalder Strasse/Senefelderplatz
www.gugelhof.de

Comfortable and friendly restaurant serving Alsatian food. A favorite of locals and tourists (including Bill Clinton). Moderate.

the story of Germany's Jews–from contributions to German society to inclusion into German life to the devastating forced exclusion.

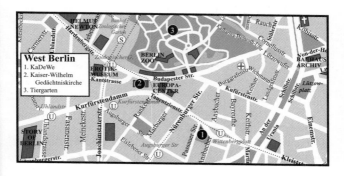

Kurfürstendamm
U-Bahn: Uhlandstrasse or Kurfürstendamm

This street (thankfully referred to as Ku'damm) is the main shopping street of what used to be West Berlin. Intersecting with Ku'damm is Fasanenstrasse, where you'll find the city's most upscale shops. You know, Gucci, Tiffany…

KaDeWe (Kaufhaus des Westens)
21-24 Tauentzienstrasse
Tel. 21210
Open Mon-Fri 10am-8pm, Sat 9:30am–8pm
U-Bahn: Kurfürstendamm
www.kadewe.de

This huge luxury shopping center has an incredible buffet-style food hall (the largest in Europe) on the sixth floor with over thirty places to eat. Don't miss it!

Kaiser-Wilhelm Gedächtniskirche
(Kaiser Wilhelm Memorial Church)

Breitscheidplatz
Tel. 2185023
Open daily 9am-7pm
Admission: Free
U-Bahn: Kurfürstendamm
www.gedaechtniskirche.com

One of the most recognizable of all of Berlin's sights. Allied bombs in the last days of World War II demolished all but a few walls and the bell tower of the Kaiser Wilhelm church, which had stood here since the late 1800s. It's a moving reminder of the destruction this city has seen. In 1961, a new octagonal-shaped church with blue stained-glass windows was built beside the ruins. There's a museum here telling the story of the old church, the bombing of the church and surrounding areas, and the construction of the new church.

Tiergarten
Open daily
Admission: Free
S-Bahn: Tiergarten

This 412-acre park is filled with walkers, runners and, in good weather, Berliners having picnics and sunbathing. There's a lovely canal here, the Landwehrkanal. At the east end of Strasse des 17. Juni (the park's main street) is the Sowjetisches Ehrenmal (Soviet War Memorial). The two tanks here are said to be the first tanks to enter Berlin at the end of the war. All the roads and paths in the park lead to another memorial, the Siegessäule (Victory Column) (in the center of Strasse des 17. Juni) commemorating Prussian military victories against France, Austria and Denmark. The Goddess of Victory tops this red-granite column. You can climb the spiral staircase to reach an observation platform with good views of the park and the surrounding area (€3).

At the north end of the park is a small palace, the Schloss Bellevue. This is the home of the German president. The modern, oval-shaped building just south of here is the Bundespräsidialamt, where Germany's president has his office. The park is a great place to get away from the bustling city. The name means "Animal Garden," as this was originally the royal hunting preserve.

Pink Village/Gay and Lesbian Berlin
U-Bahn: Nollendorfplatz
www.berlin-tourist-information.de/english/zielgruppen

Berlin has long had an active gay community. The area around the Nollendorfplatz (especially Motzstrasse) is the center of gay life. Here are a few café/bars in the area (there are also many gay establishments in Prenzlauer Berg, especially in the area around the U-Bahn Schönhauser Allee):
• Hafen, 19 Motzstrasse, Tel. 21141180 (men)
• Tom's, 19 Motzstrasse, Tel 2134570 (men)
• Begine, 139 Potsdamer Strasse, Tel. 2151414 (women)
• More, 28 Motzstrasse, Tel. 23635702 (restaurant)

BERLIN WALL WALK
Highlights: **Brandenburger Tor, Potsdamer Platz, Kulturforum** and **Checkpoint Charlie**. Distance: Approximately one-and-a-half miles. Map pages 80-81.

Between 1949 and 1961, three million people left East Berlin and East Germany. To stop this mass exodus, a 100-mile wall was built, known simply as the Berlin Wall, a barrier that remained for 28 years. The wall was 13 feet tall and had a buffer zone of between 25 and 160 feet. Ultimately, 300 guard towers were built to monitor the area near the wall. In that 28-year period, 5,043 people are known to have successfully gotten around the wall. Guards fired at 1,693 people and made 3,221 arrests. The East Germans referred to the wall as "The Anti-Fascist Protective Rampart." Although most of the wall is gone today, this walk takes you along a portion of the former wall.

We start our walk at the Unter den Linden S-Bahn stop. Head down (west) on Unter den Linden toward the triumphal arch, the Brandenburger Tor.

The square in front of the triumphal arch is Pariser Platz. The name of this square "celebrates" the German occupation of

Paris in 1814. This was ground zero for bombing by the Allies in World War II. Today, it's lined with banks, hotels, German governmental offices and embassies, including, ironically, the French Embassy. The very fancy Adlon Hotel is also here.

Now, head toward the triumphal arch.

The Brandenburger Tor (Brandenburg Gate) is probably Berlin's most recognizable sight. This famous gate was originally called the "Friedenstor" ("Gate of Peace"). Built in 1791 as a triumphal arch, it was at one time one of 18 gates in the capital

 of Prussia. The gate features six Doric columns topped by the statue of Victory driving a four-horse chariot. Badly damaged in World War II bombing, it was long in a sort of no man's land when the Berlin wall stood. When the wall came down, it was the sight of huge celebrations. It's recently been restored.

Head to the room built into the guard station (to the right as you face the gate).

The Raum der Stille (Room of Silence) allows you to quietly contemplate Berlin's turbulent history. It's meant to remind people of the original idea of the gate as a gate of peace.

Walk through the gate (with the Pariser Platz to your back).

In the distance, you can see the Siegessäule (Victory Column).

Now, turn left down Ebertstrasse to our next sight. You are now walking along the former Berlin Wall. You'll notice along this walk that the location of the former Berlin Wall is marked by a path of bricks set into the street.

On your left, just south of the Brandenburg Gate, is the construction site of the new U.S. Embassy.

Continue down the street. Our next sight is also to your left.

The **Denkmal für die Ermordeten Juden Europas** (Memorial to the Murdered European Jews) is a massive memorial of 2,700 pillars honoring Jews killed by the Nazis. Truly an impressive and thought-provoking memorial. You can also visit its underground center with information on the Holocaust. *Tel. 74072929. Open at all times. Information center open daily 10am-8pm. Admission: Free. S-Bahn: Unter den Linden. www.holocaustmahnmal.de*

Continue down Ebertstrasse.

To your right is the **Tiergarten**, Berlin's great green space right in the middle of the city.

As you continue down Ebertstrasse, to your left is a "sight" that will cause you to pause and reflect.

The location of the **Führerbunker** (Hitler's Bunker) is not marked by any signs, and the German government has specifically left it unmarked in fear that it would become a pilgrimage shrine for neo-Nazis. There's a children's playground on the spot where it's said that the bodies of Eva Braun and Adolph Hitler were burnt. Some of the bunker was destroyed by the Soviets at the end of the war, and other parts were recently discovered during a construction project. A little farther down the street on your left is the **Berlin Hi-Flyer** (across from the Marriott Hotel) where you can view the sights in a hot air balloon (€20).

Head to the large square at the end of Ebertstrasse.

Bombed beyond recognition in World War II, this square, **Potsdamer Platz**, found itself in East Berlin. Unused and undeveloped while the city was divided, after reunification, it became a huge construction site.

On the right side of the street at the intersection with Potsdamer Platz is a piece of the Berlin Wall. You'll see people taking photographs here.

Turn right at Potsdamer Platz (the sign says Potsdamer Platz, but this is also Potsdamer Strasse).

Soon on your right, you'll see the entrance for the Sony Center, a steel-and-glass entertainment complex that is home to tons of movie theaters, a dancing fountain, cafés and restaurants. The huge canopy (interestingly lit at night) is fantastic. This is also the location of the Filmmuseum Berlin (closed Mondays), devoted to the history of German film. Even if you're not a film buff, you'll find much of interest here.

After you've visited the Sony Center, exit where you came in and turn right. You're now on Potsdamer Strasse. You'll soon be at our next stop.

The Kulturforum is home to the following:
• Philharmonie: Home of the Berlin Philharmonic Orchestra.
• Staatsbibliothek: The State Library.
• Gemäldegalerie (Picture Gallery): One of the world's greatest collections of European art from the 13th to the 18th century.
• Neue Nationalgalerie (New National Gallery): Filled with works by 20th-century German and international artists.
• Kunstgewerbemuseum (Museum of Applied Arts): Arts and crafts from the past 1,000 years are on display here.
• Musikinstrumenten-Museum (Musical Instruments Museum): Filled with every imaginable musical instrument.

After visiting the Sony Center and the Kulturforum, head back to the intersection of Ebertstrasse and Potsdamer Platz. Follow Stresemannstrasse (to your right) and turn left onto Niederkirchnerstrasse.

To your right at number 7 is Martin-Gropius-Bau. Built in 1881, this beautiful renovated building features changing art exhibits.

Directly across the street is the Abgeordnetenhaus von Berlin, a building dating back to the 1890s. It was the former Prussian parliament building, and now is home to the Berlin House of Deputies.

You can see portions of the Berlin Wall running along this street (to your right). Behind this section of the Berlin Wall is our next sight.

The Prinz Albrecht Palais (the former headquarters of Hitler's Gestapo) once stood here. Today it's the Topographie des Terrors (Topography of Terror). There's an exhibit here on the history of Nazi terror.

On the left side of the street is the Bundesministerium der Finanzen (German Finance Ministry). This Nazi-era building and former home to the Nazi Air Force (Luftwaffe) survived World War II bombing. It's now the German Finance Ministry. While part of communist East Germany, it housed the Ministry of Ministries (no kidding)!

Continue down the street (the name of the street changes to Zimmerstrasse when you pass Wilhelmstrasse).

To your left at the corner of Friedrichstrasse and Zimmerstrasse is a memorial of crosses with the names of those killed attempting to flee East Berlin.

Our final stop is to your right at Friedrichstrasse (the street after Wilhelmstrasse).

Haus am Checkpoint Charlie (Checkpoint Charlie) at 43-45 Friedrichstrasse was the only checkpoint through which foreigners could pass between East and West Berlin. The history of the construction of the Berlin Wall is documented, along with incredible attempts to escape East Berlin. Attempts to escape included tunnels, hot-air balloons, a mini-submarine, cars and shopping carts! There's also a display dedicated to the Berlin Wall's demise in the 1989 peaceful revolution. *Tel. 2537250. Open daily 9am-10pm. Admission: €9.50. U-Bahn: Kochstrasse. www.mauermuseum.de.*

BERLIN GETTING THERE/GETTING AROUND
There are three airports serving Berlin, and shuttle buses run frequently between all three. Most Northern Americans arrive through Tegel (5 miles [8 km] northwest of the central city).

A taxi to the central city costs around €20 and takes 20 minutes (depending on traffic). Buses (€2) run here (X9 and 109) to the Bahnhof Zoo (in the western part of the city) every 15 minutes, with stops at major U- and S-Bahn stations. Bus TXL goes to Alexanderplatz (in the eastern part of the city), with stops at major U-Bahn and S-Bahn stations. You can take public transportation from these stops to your hotel. There's a tourist-information booth in the main terminal that can help steer you in the right direction.

Flights from other German cities (and some nearby European destinations) use Tempelhof (4 miles [6 km] southeast of the city center). Taxis cost approximately €20 to the central city. U-Bahn (Platz der Luftbrücke) or bus #109 run to the central city (approximately €3). Tempelhof's future is uncertain.

If you arrive by train at either Berlin Ostbahnhof or Bahnhof Zoologischer Garten, you can reach your final destination by taxi or S-Bahn connections. The new Lehrter Bahnhof, located conveniently in the central city, will open in 2006.

Berlin's public-transportation network is easy to use. You can change from underground (U-Bahn) to surface rail (S-Bahn), to trams (in former East Berlin only) to bus with one ticket for two hours after validation (€2). There are ticket-vending machines at each station with instructions in English. There is an office of the public-transportation system (the BVG) at the airport where you can buy your passes. You must have a validated ticket, so look for the validating machine before you get on. If you don't have a validated ticket, you're going to pay a significant fine (€40). Believe me, they do check! A day ticket costs €5.60. A 7-day-ticket costs €24.30.

The WelcomeCard costs €16 (for two consecutive days) and €22 (for three days), and provides discounts to certain museums and tours and free public transportation within Berlin. It's available at tourist-information centers.

VENICE

A serene world of elegant decay "floating" in a lagoon, Venice is unlike anywhere else in the world. Despite the tourists, the sometimes aromatic canals and the often inflated prices, Venice continues to be a dream destination. Many cities claim to be pedestrian-only, but Venice truly is car-free. Don't just take a day trip here. Once the day trippers leave, Venice becomes a quiet, romantic maze of streets with spectacular architecture. As many times as I have visited, I am always amazed by its beauty. If you can, visit Venice in the off-season so you can experience the quieter side of this incredible city.

Canal Grande
(Grand Canal)

Winding its way for two miles through the city, the Grand Canal, Venice's "main street," isn't a street at all. Lined with colorful *palazzos*, the canal is a highlight for all visitors to Venice. You can ride in a *gondola* (make sure you know the price before boarding), a water taxi (even pricier), or the *vaporetti*, the water buses that are the main way to get around. For €5, hop on #1 (it stops at each *vaporetto* stop) and take a 45-minute tour of the Grand Canal. Try to get a seat up front for the best views (but don't stand up there or you'll be asked to move so the driver can see).

Take #82 for a faster trip down the Grand Canal with fewer stops. Note that some *vaporetti* finish at the Rialto Bridge. They're marked "Solo Rialto." If you want to get on and off, buy a 24-hour card for €11. You can purchase tickets at the ticket booth at the stop or on board (but buy it from the conductor as soon as you board).

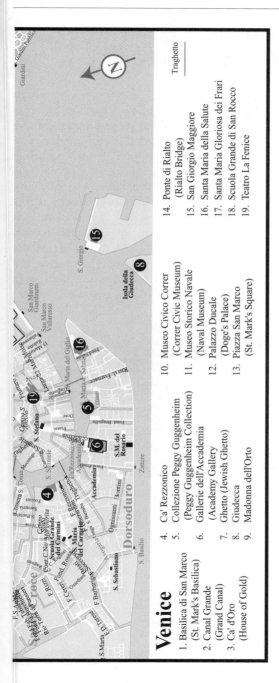

Venice

1. Basilica di San Marco
   (St. Mark's Basilica)
2. Canal Grande
   (Grand Canal)
3. Ca' d'Oro
   (House of Gold)
4. Ca' Rezzonico
5. Collezione Peggy Guggenheim
   (Peggy Guggenheim Collection)
6. Gallerie dell'Accademia
   (Academy Gallery)
7. Ghetto (Jewish Ghetto)
8. Giudecca
9. Madonna dell'Orto
10. Museo Civico Correr
    (Correr Civic Museum)
11. Museo Storico Navale
    (Naval Museum)
12. Palazzo Ducale
    (Doge's Palace)
13. Piazza San Marco
    (St. Mark's Square)
14. Ponte di Rialto
    (Rialto Bridge)
15. San Giorgio Maggiore
16. Santa Maria della Salute
17. Santa Maria Gloriosa dei Frari
18. Scuola Grande di San Rocco
19. Teatro La Fenice

Traghetto

Take the Traghetto!

A *gondola* ride costs up to €100 for less than an hour ride (more in the evening). I like to get on a *traghetto*. These large *gondolas* take you across the Grand Canal for less than €1. It's a fun way to experience a *gondola* ride for a fraction of the cost. And since there are only three bridges that cross the Grand Canal, this can also save you lots of time walking to the nearest one.

Piazza San Marco
(St. Mark's Square)
Vaporetto: San Marco

This vast square is the heart of Venice. Although it can be packed during the day with both tourists and pigeons, if you come here at night or in early morning you'll have one of the most fabulous locations in the world nearly all to yourself in the eerie mist and fog. The square is home to Caffè Florian. This elegant and expensive café has been in business since 1720, and it's worth the splurge to sit and listen to the orchestra music.

Overlooking it all is the Campanile San Marco (St. Mark's Bell Tower), where you can take an elevator to the top for great views. Admission: €6, open daily 9am-7pm (until 9pm in summer). As you face the basilica, the small square to your

right (connecting St. Mark's Square with the Grand Canal) is the equally lovely Piazzetta San Marco. To your left as you face the basilica is the Torre dell'Orologio (Clock Tower) dating back to the mid-1400s. Two "Moors" strike the bell on the hour.

This is also the entry to the Mercerie, a retail area filled with touristy eateries, souvenir shops and high-end boutiques. Travelers continue to flock to Harry's Bar on Calle Vallaresso (just west of St. Mark's Square). Although dinner is extremely expensive (and many complain not worth the cost), most come to have a martini or delicious *Bellini* (sparkling *Prosecco* wine and peach juice) at the bar.

Basilica di San Marco
(St. Mark's Basilica)
Piazza San Marco
Tel. 041/5225205
Open Mon-Sat 9:30am-5pm, Sun 2pm-4pm
Admisson: Free to basilica. Treasury (Tesoro): €2. Pala d'Oro and Sanctuary (Santuario): €1.50. Galleria and Museum: €3
Vaporetto: San Marco

Under the five domes of this sumptuous, candlelit basilica, you'll find some of the world's most amazing mosaics. The oldest are in the atrium, and are scenes from the Old Testament. The basilica is said to house the bones of St. Mark, brought here in the 800s, and the mosaic above the far left door tells the story. The basilica is laid out in the form of a Greek cross. It's called the *Chiesa d'Oro* (Golden Church), as it's filled with riches pilfered from the Orient, many of which are housed in the treasury (*tesoro*).

Highlights of the basilica are the Pala d'Oro, a golden altar screen embellished with hundreds of jewels. Upstairs is the Galleria and Museum, where you'll not only find great views of St. Mark's Square but also the Triumphal Quadriga, four bronze horses dating back to the time of Alexander the Great in the 4th century. Note that you must be dressed appropriately to enter the basilica (no shorts, no bare shoulders).

Palazzo Ducale
(Doge's Palace)
Piazzetta San Marco
Tel. 041/2715911 (museum). 041/5209070 (tour reservations)
Open daily Nov-Mar 9am-5pm (Apr-Oct until 7pm)
Admission: €11. Secret Itinerary Tour: €13
Vaporetto: San Marco

The office of the doge was instituted in Venice around 700, and the elected doge served for life. This white-and-pink-marble palace, located next to the basilica, dates back to the early 1300s. Not only was it the doge's home, it also contained government meeting chambers and a prison. Near the basilica is the ornate Porta della Carta (Gate of the Paper), dating back to the 15th century, where official decrees were posted. Enter the palace from the waterfront, and you'll soon be climbing the Scala dei Giganti (Giants' Stairway), overseen by the large Neptune and Mars statues. Some highlights are:

• Sala di Anti-Collegio, home to *Rape of Europa* by Veronese.
• Sala del Senato, with *Triumph of Venice* by Tintoretto.
• Sala del Maggiore Consiglio, featuring *Paradise* by Tintoretto, the largest oil painting in the world.

The palace is separated from the cells of the Prigioni Nuove (New Prisons) by a small canal. Over that canal is the Ponte dei Sospiri (Bridge of Sighs), said to have been given its name because the prisoners who walked over it on their way to the cells on the other side would be seeing the beautiful lagoon, the island of San Giorgio, and freedom for the last time.

The "Secret Itinerary" tour takes you through the private apartment of the doge and secret passageways.

Museo Civico Correr
(Correr Civic Museum)
Piazza San Marco (west end of the square)
Tel 041/2405211
Open daily 9am-5pm (Apr-Oct until 7pm)
Admission: €11 (includes admission to the Ducal Palace)
Vaporetto: San Marco

Walking in Venice

When the tides roll in, low-lying sections of Venice become flooded (especially St. Mark's Square). The city sets up raised wooden planks so that you don't have to wade through the water. Also, chances are that you *will* get lost, but that's part of the beauty of visiting this wonderful place. To help you find your way, yellow signs point to major sights like the Rialto Bridge and San Marco.

Works from the 14th to 16th centuries are featured in this museum. You'll find everything from neo-Classical sculpture to silly shoes worn by the Venetians in the 16th century.

Teatro La Fenice
Campo San Fantin
Tel. 041/786511

It was at this elegant opera house that Verdi's *La Traviata* was first performed (it bombed). It was destroyed by fire in 1773 and again in a suspicious fire in 1996. It reopened in 2004. See *www.teatrolafenice.it* for a schedule of events.

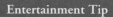

Entertainment Tip

For ten days before Ash Wednesday, Venice celebrates Carnevale, a huge party throughout the city. Need a mask for the celebration? Try Mondonovo, *Rio Terrà Canal, Dorsoduro 3063. Tel. 041/5287344,* the most famous mask-maker in Venice.

San Giorgio Maggiore
Isola San Giorgio Maggiore (across the canal from St. Mark's Square)
prison
Tel. 041/5227827
Open daily 7:30am-12:30pm and 2:30pm-6pm
Admission: Free. Bell Tower: €3
Vaporetto: San Giorgio (reached from St. Mark's by taking #82 from the San Zaccaria Jolanda stop)

Look across the waterfront from St. Mark's Square and you'll see the majestic dome and tall campanile (bell tower) of this church. Two of Tintoretto's works are here: *The Last Supper* and *Gathering of Manna*. You can take the elevator to the top of the bell tower for a panoramic view of the city.

Ca' Rezzonico
Fondamenta Rezzonico, Dorsoduro 3136
Tel. 041/2410100
Open Wed-Mon 10am-5pm (Apr-Oct until 6pm). Closed Tue
Admission: €7
Vaporetto: Ca' Rezzonico

This 17th-century *palazzo* with great views of the Grand Canal is stuffed with 18th-century Venetian art, tapestries, period furnishings, frescoes, and chandeliers.

Ponte di Rialto
(Rialto Bridge)
Vaporetto: Rialto

This stone bridge, one of three bridges crossing the Grand Canal, is the best place to see boat traffic. Great photo opportunity!

Food & Restaurant Tips

Venice has a wonderful food market at the west end of the Rialto Bridge (Rialto vaporetto). Open 7am–1pm, Mon–Sat. Near the market are a few places to try *cicheti*, the Venice version of *tapas*. Other good places in this area are:

OSTERIA ALLA BOTTE
5482 Calle della Bissa (east end of the Rialto Bridge near Campo San Bartolomeo). Tel. 041/5209775. Closed Thu and Sun

OSTERIA SORA AL PONTE
1588 Ponte delle Beccarie (near the Rialto Bridge Market off of Campo de la Beccarie). Tel. 041/718208. Closed Mon

BANCOGIRO
122 Campo San Giacometto (west end of Rialto Bridge along the Grand Canal). Tel. 041/5232061. Closed Sun (dinner) and Mon

Ca' d'Oro
(House of Gold)
Calle Ca' d'Oro, Cannaregio 3933
Tel. 041/5200345
Open Tue-Sun 8:15pm-7:15pm (Mon until 2pm)
Admission: €11
Vaporetto: Ca' d'Oro

This fabulous building is just as much an attraction as the collection of art it houses. Highlights include its beautiful courtyard and views of the Grand Canal. Among the treasures inside is the painting *Venus* by Titian.

Scuola Grande di San Rocco
Campo San Rocco, San Polo 3052
Tel. 041/5234864
Open daily 10am-4pm (Apr-Oct until 5:30pm)
Admission: €6
Vaporetto: San Tomà

Filled with nearly 60 large religious paintings by Tintoretto, this sumptuous hall is sometimes called "Tintoretto's Sistine Chapel."

Santa Maria Gloriosa dei Frari
Campo dei Frari, San Polo
Tel. 041/2750462
Open Mon-Sat 9am-6pm, Sun 1pm-6pm
Admission: €6
Vaporetto: San Tomà

This huge Gothic church is filled with incredible works of art, including Titian's *Assumption* (over the main altar) and *Madonna Enthroned* (first altar to the right after you enter); Donatello's wood carving of St. John the Baptist (to the right of the main altar); and Bellini's *Madonna and Child with Saints* (in the sacristy).

Santa Maria della Salute
Campo della Salute, Dorsoduro
Tel. 041/5237591
Open daily 9am-noon and 3pm-5:30pm (Apr-Sep until 6:30pm)
Admission: Free. Sacristy: €2
Vaporetto: Salute

This church, with its huge dome, is dedicated to the Virgin Mary for saving the city from a plague that killed thousands of Venetians in 1630. The Sacristy contains works by Titian, and Tintoretto's *The Wedding at Cana*.

Gallerie dell'Accademia
(Academy Gallery)
Campo della Carità, Dorsoduro 1050
Tel. 041/5222247
Open Tue-Sun 8:15am-7:15pm (Mon until 2pm)
Admission: €7
Vaporetto: Accademia

An incredible collection of Venetian art spanning the 13th to 18th centuries, including works by Bellini, Carpaccio, Tintoretto, Veronese and Titian.

Collezione Peggy Guggenheim
(Peggy Guggenheim Collection)
Fondamenta Venier dei Leoni, Dorsoduro 701
Tel. 041/2405411
Open Wed-Mon 10am-6pm. Closed Tue
Admission: €10
Vaporetto: Accademia (then follow signs)

The 20th-century art collection of heiress Peggy Guggenheim is housed in her former Grand Canal retirement *palazzo*. You'll find works by Picasso, Dalí, Chagall, Klee, Pollock and Kandinsky, to name a few. Lovely garden.

Ghetto
(Jewish Ghetto)
Vaporetto: San Marcuola or Ponte Guglie

In the early 1500s, Jews were confined to an island in the Cannaregio district named after its *geto* (Venetian for "foundry"). This neighborhood of narrow streets is still home to Jewish establishments and five synagogues built in the 16th century.

The Museo Ebraico celebrates the neighborhood's Jewish history, and offers tours of the synagogues and the neighborhood in both Italian and English. *Campo Ghetto Nuovo, Cannaregio 2902/b. Tel. 041/715359. Open Jun-Sep Sun-Fri 10am-7pm, last tour at 5:30pm (Oct-May until 6pm, last tour at 4:30pm). Admission: €3 (museum), €9 (tour).*

Madonna dell'Orto
Campo dell'Orto, Cannaregio 3512
Tel. 041/2750462
Open Mon-Sat 10am-5pm, Sun 1pm-5pm. Closed Sun Jul-Aug
Admission: €3
Vaporetto: Madonna dell'Orto

Tintoretto is buried in this Gothic church at the northern end of the city. The main altar features two of his works: *Sacrifice of the Golden Calf* (to the left), and *Last Judgment* (to the right). (By the way, the Cannaregio is a great neighborhood to stroll and get away from the crowds.)

Giudecca
Vaporetto: Zitelle, Redentore or Palanca

This island is both a working-class neighborhood and the location of one of the most exclusive hotels in the world: the Cipriani.

Museo Storico Navale
(Naval Museum)
Campo San Biagio, Castello 2148
Tel. 041/5200276
Open Mon-Fri 8:45am-1:30pm (Sat until 1pm)
Admission: €2
Vaporetto: Arsenale

This museum celebrates Venice's naval history and has an impressive boat collection. (I personally like the collection of seashells.) Nearby is the huge Arsenale shipyard.

Excursions Around the Venetian Lagoon
Boats depart from the San Zaccaria stop near St. Mark's Square. There are also departures for Murano, Burano, Torcello, and San Michele from the Fondamenta Nuove stop in Cannaregio.

Each island in the lagoon offers something different for the traveler.

Murano: Sort of like a little Venice with its own Grand Canal

Restaurant Tips around Venice

AVOGARIA

1629 Dorsoduro. Calle della Avogaria (near Campo San Sebastiano), Tel. 041/2960491, Closed Tue, Vaporetto: San Basilio

Modern, sleek decor and southern Italian cuisine. You can also sit at the small bar and have appetizers. There's a small courtyard used in warm weather. Fun, friendly and worth the hike. Moderate.

AI GONDOLIERI

366 Fondamenta dell'Ospedaleto (near the Guggenheim Museum at Fondamenta Venier dai Leoni), Tel. 041/5286396, Closed Tue, Vaporetto: Accademia

Not for seafood lovers. This restaurant serves meat dishes. Delicious *fiori di zucca* (zucchini flowers filled w/cheese, then battered and fried). Moderate-Expensive.

DA IVO

1809 San Marco. Calle dei Fuseri (near Campo S. Luca), Tel. 041/5285004, Closed Sun and Jan Vaporetto: San Marco

Beautiful restaurant serving Venetian and Tuscan specialties. Try the delicious *bistecca alla Fiorentina* (T-bone steak). Expensive-Very Expensive.

VINO VINO

2007A San Marco. Ponte delle Veste (between La Fenice and via XXII Marzo), Tel. 041/2417688, Closed Tue, Vaporetto: S. Maria del Giglio

Popular wine bar and restaurant serving typical Venetian cuisine and offering 350 Italian and imported wines. Inexpensive.

ENOTECA AL VOLTO

4081 San Marco. Calle Cavalli (between the Grand Canal and Salizzada San Luca), Tel. 041/5228945 Closed Sun, No credit cards, Vaporetto: Rialto

This wine bar has wooden tables and chairs, wine labels as wallpaper, an impressive wine list, and simple Venetian fare. A great deal. Inexpensive.

and islands connected by picturesque bridges. The famous glassworks are located here, and you can visit them to watch glass being handblown by artisans.

Burano: Brightly painted houses and lots of shops selling lace. You can visit the **Museo del Merletto** (Lace Museum) to see women creating lovely handmade (and expensive) lace (closed Tuesdays).

Torcello: Come here if you want to get away from it all. This nearly deserted island (less than twenty people live here) has a church with a small museum, but not much else.

San Michele: Venice's island cemetery.

Lido: Once one of *the* places to be seen, the Lido and its beaches have now seen better days. It still draws tourists to its luxury hotels and casino, but you won't find many swimming in the polluted waters.

VENICE GETTING THERE/GETTING AROUND

A two-mile-long causeway connects Venice with modern and bland Mestre on the coast. If you arrive by car, the road ends at a parking lot on the edge of the island (Autorimessa Comunale, Garage San Marco, or Tronchetto), costing about €20 per day. When you leave the car park or train station, you'll be right at the Grand Canal where you can board a *vaporetto* (water bus). See Grand Canal entry above for more information. You may want to store excess bags at the train station, because Venice is a nightmare for heavy packers trying to lug their bags over bridges and along narrow streets.

Marco Polo Airport is six miles north of Venice. You can take a water taxi to your hotel (easiest and most expensive) beginning at €80. **Buses** connect the airport with the Piazzale Roma *vaporetto* (water bus) stop for €3 (blue ATVO bus). You can then get on a *vaporetto* to reach your final destination. The Alilaguna **speedboats** also connect the airport to St. Mark's Square (€11 per person). The airport tourist information can help you with all these connections.

ROME

Rome is a magical city, where each step you take is a walk through history: ancient ruins set against the glory of Renaissance churches, complemented by museums overflowing with stunning relics and incomparable works of art. Because there is so much to see and do, the chief difficulty most visitors have in Rome is that even a month's worth of concentrated touring will only scratch the surface. So, if your time is limited, here are Rome's must-see sights, as well as some top-notch cafés and restaurants.

Vatican Museums
Viale Vaticano
Tel. 06/6988-4466
From Nov-Mar and June-Aug open 8:45am-12:20pm. Mar-June and Sep-Oct open 8:45am -3:20pm. Closed most Sun and all religious holidays
Admission: €12. Free the last Sun of every month in Jan, Feb, Apr, May, July, Aug, Sep, Oct, Nov and Dec
Web: www.vatican.va
Metro: Ottaviano

The Vatican Museums keep rather short hours, and do not take reservations. If you want to avoid walking long distances or standing in lines, choose a tour company and make a reservation to join a private group tour in English. There are also a number of self-guided, tape-cassette tours.

Pinacoteca Vaticana: A wonderful collection of masterpieces from many periods, including paintings by Giotto and Raphael, the famous Brussels Tapestries, and countless other religious-themed works.

Pius Clementine Museum: Known mainly as a sculpture

museum, you can also find mosaics and sarcophagi from the 2nd, 3rd and 4th centuries.

Chiaramonti Museum: This museum includes a collection of over 5,000 pagan and Christian works.

Etruscan Museum: Relics of the civilization that preceded ancient Rome. The museum contains objects excavated from southern Etruria between 1828-1836, as well as pieces from later excavations around Rome.

Egyptian Museum: A valuable documentary of the art and civilization of ancient Egypt.

Library of the Vatican: The library contains over 500,000 volumes, including the valuable a 4th-century Bible in Greek.

Appartamento Borgia: Funded by Pope Alexander VI (whose family name was Borgia). From the furnishings to the paintings to the frescoes of Isis and Osiris on the ceiling, this little "museum" is worth a look.

Sistine Chapel: The private chapel of the popes, famous for its ceiling painted by Michelangelo. Started in 1508 and finished four years later, the ceiling depicts scenes from the Bible, including *Creation of Adam*, *Creation of Eve*, the *Fall and the Expulsion from Paradise*, the *Sacrifice of Noah and his Family*, and the *Deluge*. The great fresco on the wall behind the altar of the *Last Judgment* is also by Michelangelo, and was commissioned by Clement VII when Michelangelo was over 60 years old.

Rooms of Raphael: Pope Julius II loved the work of Raphael so much, he commissioned the artist to paint the entire room himself. Not nearly as stupendous as Michelangelo's Sistine Chapel, but it's still one of the world's masterpieces.

Chapel of Nicholas V: Decorated with frescoes from 1448-1451 by Giovanni da Fiesole, representing scenes from the lives of Saint Stephan and Saint Lawrence.

The Loggia of Raphael: Divided into 13 arcades with 48 scenes from the Old and New Testaments, executed from designs of Raphael by his students.

San Pietro–Saint Peter's
Piazza San Pietro
Tel. 06/6988-4466
Open 8am-6pm (until 5pm in winter)
Metro: Ottaviano

Saint Peter's is a Bernini masterpiece and the largest church in the world. (Note: One of the best ways to see St. Peter's is on a free English-language guided tour available seven days a week, Monday-Saturday at 3pm and Sundays at 2:30pm. The one-hour tour offers an in-depth historical and religious perspective of this magnificent church. Tours start at the information desk to the right as you enter the portico. *For more information, call 06/6972.*)

The church is filled with masterpieces, including

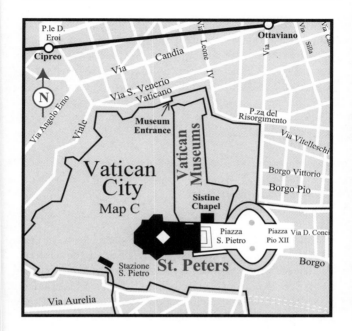

Michelangelo's world-famous *Pieta*, sculpted when the artist was only 24. And don't miss the statue of **Saint Peter**, whose toes have been rubbed so many times for good luck that they've all but disappeared.

Just past the statue of St. Peter is Michelangelo's **Grand Cupola**, one of the most amazing architectural wonders of all time. Below the cupola, rising above the high altar, is Bernini's **Grand Canopy**. And the **Chapel of Confessions** by Maderno is in front of the altar, around which 95 perpetually lit lamps illuminate the **Tomb of Saint Peter**.

Throughout the rest of the basilica you'll find extraordinary statues and monuments, many papal tombs—including the tomb of Pope Celestine V who allegedly died at the hands of his overeager successor, Boniface VIII; recent x-rays clearly show a 10-inch nail driven into Celestine's skull—and a wealth of chapels, including the lovely **Gregorian Chapel**, also designed by Michelangelo.

There are literally thousands of eye-catching wonders to experience inside the church. But if at any time you get overwhelmed by the sheer quantity, you can always ascend into the cupola either by stairs (537 of them), or by elevator, to enjoy the magnificent bird's-eye views of the city.

The Capitoline Museums
Piazza del Campidoglio 1
Tel. 06/6710-2071
Open Tue-Sun 9am-7pm. Closed Mon
Admission: €6
Web: www.museicapitolini.it
Metro: Colosseo

The place to see what ancient Romans looked like, warts and all. (Unlike Greek sculpture, which glorified the subject, Roman sculpture captured every realistic characteristic and flaw.) Besides portrait busts, you'll find a variety of celebrated pieces from antiquity, including the *Dying Gaul*, *Cupid and Psyche*, the *Faun*, and the voluptuous *Capitoline Venice*. The Room of the Doves contains two wonderful mosaics taken from Hadrian's Villa. The Palace of the Conservatori, constructed from a design by Michelangelo, consists of three distinct collections: the Museum of the Conservatori, the New Museum, and the Pinocoteca Capitolina. Here you'll find the huge stone head, hand and foot from a statue of Constantine. Look for the *She-Wolf of the Capitol*, an Etruscan work of Romulus and Remus being suckled by the mythical wolf of Rome; the death mask bust of Michelangelo; the marble Medusa head by Bernini; the celebrated painting of *St. Sebastian* by Guido Reni; and the famous Caravaggio work, *St. John the Baptist*.

Roman Forum & Palatine Hill
Largo Romolo e Remo 1
Tel. 06/699-0110
Open 9am- 8pm and in the summers on Sat until midnight
Admission: €8
www.roma2000.it/zforo.html
Metro: Colosseo

Lying between the Palatine and Quirinale hills, the Roman Forum was first a burial ground for the early settlers of the area, then became the center for religious, commercial and political activities. The entire area has been decimated by war, used as a quarry for other buildings in Rome, and has been haphazardly excavated, but is still a wonder to behold. You'll find the following sights:

- Arch of Septimus Severus
- Rostra
- Temple of Saturn
- Basilica Giulia
- Basilica Emilia
- The Curia
- Temple of Anthony & Faustina
- Temple of Caesar
- Temple of Castor & Pollux
- House of the Vestal Virgins
- Arch of Titus
- Temple of Romulus
- Basilica of Maxentius

The Palatine Hill

Of the Seven Hills of Rome, the ancient structures on this one have not fallen victim to modern progress. Once the residence of the Roman emperors, it was here, in 754 B.C., that Romulus is said to have founded the city of Rome. However, actual records have indicated that the settlement was actually established in the 9th century B.C. Aristocratic families also resided here, leaving behind wonderful architectural relics. Entering the Palatine, you pass through the Farnese Gardens.

Underneath the gardens is the Cryptoporticus, a subterranean tunnel built by Nero. Further up the hill is the Domus Livia, named after Augustus's wife. The wall paintings here date from the late Republic period. Nearby is the Domus Flavia, with the ruins of what appears to be a maze. Next to that is the Domus Augustana, the emperor's private residence. In between the Domus Flavia and Domus Augustana is the Palatine Museum, which houses human remains and artifacts from the earliest communities in Rome. Finally, at the farthest corner of the Palatine lie the remains of the small palace and baths of

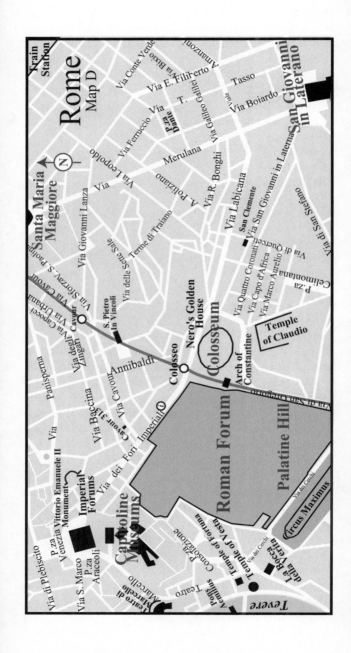

Septimus Severus, some of the best-preserved buildings on the hill.

Colosseum
Piazza del Colosseo
Tel. 06/3996-7700
Open 9am-7pm (until 5pm in winter)
Admission: €8
Web: www.roma2000.it/zcoloss.html
Metro: Colosseo

The Colosseum (Flavian Amphitheater) remains the single most recognized monument from ancient Rome. Over 500 exotic beasts and many hundreds of gladiators were slain in the arena during the building's opening ceremony in 80 A.D., which lasted three months. The structure was severely damaged by an earthquake in the 5th century A.D. and saw some use afterwards as a theater. Since then it has been used as a fortress and as a quarry.

Pantheon
Piazza della Rotonda
Tel. 06/ 6830-0230
Open Mon- Sat 9am-6:30pm, Sun 9am-1pm. Mass at 10am on Sun
Web: www.roma2000.it/zpanthe.html
Buses: 70, 81, 87, 90

Constructed in 27 B.C., the Pantheon is made up of red and gray Egyptian granite, and each of its columns is composed of a single block of stone. You enter the building by way of the original bronze doors. The marvelous dome is inspiring, even with the hole in the middle. There are four tombs in the building, including the tomb of an artist whose last name of Sanzio is not nearly as well-known as his first: Raphael.

Piazza Navona
Buses: 70, 81, 87, 90

This popular piazza is on the site of a stadium built in A.D. 86 that was used for mock naval battles, gladiatorial contests, and horse races. The stadium's old north entrance has been excavated, exposing some original stone arches located 20 feet below the current street level. Today the style of the piazza is richly Baroque. In the middle of the square is Bernini's Fontana Dei Quattro Fiumi (Fountain of Four Rivers), depicting the four major rivers known at the time: the Danube, the Ganges, the Nile, and the Plata.

Notice the figure representing the Nile shielding its eyes from the facade of the church it's facing, Santa Agnese in Agone. The church was designed by Bernini's rival, Borromini; and Bernini is playfully showed his disdain for his rival's design through the sculpted disgust in his statue. The piazza is also home to a fun Christmas fair that lasts from mid-December to mid-January.

San Giovanni in Laterano
Piazza San Giovanni in Laterano 4
Tel. 06/6988-6452
Open: Baptistery 6am-12:30pm and 4pm-7pm; Cloisters 9am-5pm
Web: www.roma2000.it/zschgiov.html
Metro: San Giovanni

Another great basilica. Most people don't realize that this church, and not St. Peter's, is the cathedral of Rome and the whole Catholic world. To get inside, you must pass through the bronze door that used to be attached to the old Roman Senate house. The interior of the church is laid out in the form of a Latin cross. The most beautiful artistic aspect of the church is the vast transept, richly decorated with marbles and frescoes portraying the Leggenda Aurea of Constantine.

Santa Maria Maggiore
Piazza di Santa Maria Maggiore
Tel. 06/483-195

Open 8am-7pm
Web: www.roma2000.it/ zschmar.html
Metro: Termini

This is one of the four patriarchal basilicas of Rome. Its name derives from being the largest (*maggiore*) church in the city dedicated to Mary. The façade is nothing to look at, but the interior is worth a visit, mainly because of the 5th-century mosaics, definitely the best in Rome, its frescoes, and multicolored marble. The church is home to the Borghese Chapel, so called since the vaults of the wealthy Borghese family lie beneath it. And Pius VI's eerie crypt is below and in front of the main altar.

Piazza di Spagna
Metro: Spagna

Built in the 17th century, this is one of the most beautiful gathering spots in Rome. Named after the old Spanish Embassy to the Holy See, the 137 steps are officially called the Scalinata della Trinita dei Monti, but most people just call them the

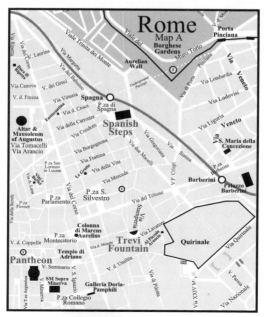

Spanish Steps. The fountain in the middle of the piazza is the **Barcaccia**, designed by Bernini in commemoration of the big flood of 1598. To the right is the column of the Immaculate Conception, erected in 1865 by Pius IX.

Trevi Fountain
Piazza di Trevi
Metro: Barberini

The largest and most impressive of Rome's fountains, taking up an entire exterior wall of the **Palazzo Poli**. In the central niche is Neptune on his chariot, drawn by marine horses preceded by two tritons. In the left niche is the statue representing Abundance, and to the right Health. The four statues on top depict the seasons. There is an ancient custom that guarantees that all who throw a coin into the fountain are destined to return to the city. When in Rome ...

Restaurant Tips around Rome

LA BUCA DI RIPETTA
Via di Ripetta 36, Tel. 06/321-9391
Metro: Flaminio

This small local trattoria serves great Roman cuisine. With its high walls covered with cooking and farming paraphernalia, the atmosphere complements the great food. You simply must dine here. Moderate.

SORA LELLA
Via di Ponte IV Capi 16, Tel. 06/686-1601
Closed Sun

Great food and atmosphere in a unique location. Expensive

VINI E BUFFET
Piazza della Torretta 60, Tel 06/687-1445
Closed Sun

A characteristic Roman eatery with friendly staff, excellent food and an extensive wine list. Inexpensive

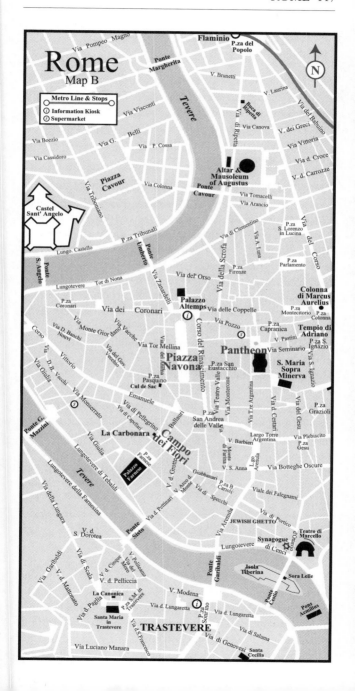

Campo dei Fiori
Buses: 46, 62, 64, 65, 70

This typically Roman piazza hosts a lively flower and food market every morning until 1pm, except Sundays. Here you'll hear the cries of vendors blending with the bargaining of the customers. The majority of the stands are for the locals, as are the majority of the shoppers, so it's a perfect place to catch a glimpse of authentic Roman life.

ROME GETTING THERE/GETTING AROUND

Most travelers will arrive at Rome's Fiumicino (Leonardo da Vinci) Airport. You also may arrive at Rome's Ciampino airport. The website for both of Rome's airports is: *www.adr.it*. Rome's Fiumicino has a dedicated train to whisk you directly to Rome's central train station (Stazione Termini). The trip costs €9 one way and takes 30 minutes. There are trains every half-hour that start operating from the airport to Termini at 7:38am and end at 10:08pm. When the train arrives at Termini, you catch a taxi to your hotel from the taxi stand in front of the station. You can also hop on the Metro, which is underneath the station, or take one of the many city buses located outside the front of the building.

If you fly into Rome's Ciampino (which is really only used for flights from European counties), there are dedicated airport buses that leave for the Anagnina Metro Station every half-hour. Buses leave from the airport starting at 6:00am and end at 10:30pm. The only other option for both airports is taking a taxi (though beware since these will cost an arm and a leg) or taking an Airport Shuttle. Airport Shuttle, *Tel. 06/4201- 4507, Web: www.airportshuttle.it, Email: airportshuttle@airportshuttle.it.* Airport Connection Services, *Tel. 06/338-3221. Web: www.airportconnection.it. Email: airpcnn@tin.it.*

The Metro (subway) has two lines (Linea A and Linea B) that intersect below Termini station. You'll find these and all other stations marked with signs featuring a prominent white "M" inside a red square. The Metro runs from 5:30am to 11:30pm and is really crowded during rush hour. It's best to have a ticket in hand when you head down to the Metro since the machines that dispense tickets are, in true Italian fashion, usually out of service. So, get a ticket at a *tabacchi* or newsstand before coming to the Metro. These cost €1. Before entering the Metro, you will need to stamp these tickets in the yellow stamp machines at the turnstiles. The ticket is valid for one trip.

FLORENCE

A visit to Italy is not complete without a trip to Firenze—Florence—one of the most beautiful cities in the world. The Renaissance reached the height of artistic expression here, when countless master artists, writers, inventors, political theorists and artisans filled the city with their brilliant creations. Strolling through the cobblestone streets of Florence is like being in a history book come to life. The sights, smells, and sounds of this wonderful city must be experienced first-hand to appreciate and fully understand the magical atmosphere.

Accademia Museum
Via Ricasoli 60
Tel. 055/214-375
www.sbas.firenze.it/accademia
Open 9am-7pm Tue-Sat
Sun 9am-1pm
Closed Mon. Admission: €6.

Started from a discarded block of marble that Michelangelo bought on his own – no one commissioned this work – he finished sculpting *David* at the age of 25 in the year 1504, after four years of labor.

Also here is Michelangelo's *The Prisoners*, so-called because the figures appear to be trapped in stone. Designed to hold the Tomb of Pope Giulio II on their sculpted shoulders, Michelangelo died before he could bring the figures to life; now they appear as if they are struggling to be freed from the marble's embrace.

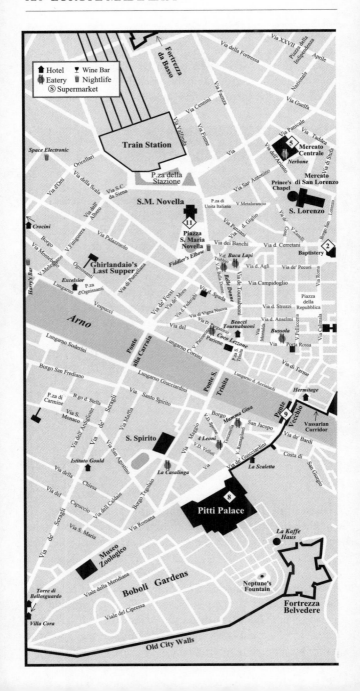

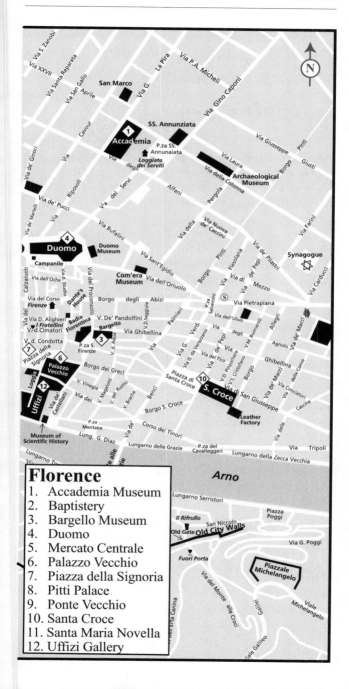

Florence

Baptistery
Piazza del Duomo
Tel. 055/230-2885
Open daily 2pm-5:30pm. Admission: €2.

Considered one of the most important buildings in the city, the Baptistery was built on the remains of an early Roman structure in the 10th and 11th centuries and dedicated to Saint John the Baptist, the patron saint of Florence. The interior is encrusted with stunning Byzantine-style mosaics. The most famous of which is the demon eating the damned to the right of the large Christ figure.

The Baptistery's octagonal shape is covered with colored marble on the outside. But the true masterpieces are the bronze paneled doors by Ghiberti. Michelangelo described the East Door by Ghiberti as "the door to paradise." When the originals were washed free during the flood of 1966 and almost lost, copies were made which is what you see now. The originals are in the Museum of the Duomo.

Bargello Museum
Via del Proconsolo
Tel 055/210-801
www.sbas.firenze.it/bargello.
Open Tues-Sat 9am-2pm and Sun 9am-1pm. Holidays 8:30am-1:50pm. Closed Mon. Admission: €4.

Located almost behind the Palazzo Signoria in the quaint Piazza S. Firenze, the Bargello houses one of the most important collections of Renaissance art and artifacts in the world. After entering into the small area called Torre Volognana, you are ushered into the *Cortile*

Restaurant Tip

BUCA LAPI
Via del Trebbio 1, Tel. 055/ 213-768. Closed Sun.
Moderate.
On a small street, down in the basement of an old building, Buca Lapi treats you to the food of a lifetime (and the spectacle of one too). There is a small open kitchen surrounded on two sides by tables from which you can see all the food being prepared. The decor is bizarre in a fun way, with travel posters covering the walls and ceiling.

(courtyard) complete with a fountain and six marble statues. Elsewhere in the museum you will find some beautiful works by Michelangelo, including *Bacco* (1496-97) and *David-Apollo* (1530-32), which is the first large classical sculpture by the artist, and *Bruto* (1530), which means ugly, and is the only bust created by Michelangelo of Lorenzo di Medici. On this floor are also some beautiful bronze statues by a variety of artists.

On the second floor are some interesting bronze animal sculptures including the famous *Tacchino* (turkey) made by Giambologna. The other featured artist in the museum is Donatello, whose works are displayed in the Salone del Consiglio Generale. The Accademia and the Uffizi get all the press, but this is one of the best museums of sculpture anywhere in the world.

Duomo
Piazza del Duomo
Tel. 055/230-2885
Church open Mon-Sat 10am-5pm, Sun 1pm-5pm. Free. Admission to the dome: €6.

Florence's cathedral is a don't miss sight. It was consecrated in 1436 by Pope Eugenio IV as Santa Maria del Fiore (Saint Mary of the Flowers). Started in 1296, by 1421 everything else was finished except for the dome. Eventually Brunelleschi won a competition to design and build the dome, beating out his Ghiberti, the creator of the bronze panels on the east door of the Baptistery.

This started a heated rivalry that some say helped spark the Renaissance itself. It took 14 years just to construct the gigantic dome, and until the Houston Astrodome was built in the 1960s, this was the largest free-standing dome in the world. The dome is not only an architectural masterpiece but is a wonder of engineering as well. Brunelleschi had to invent countless machines, pulleys, and supports just to construct the dome. Many of the designs for machinery found in **Leonardo da Vinci's** notebooks are actually sketches of actual devices created by Brunelleschi.

The dome is decorated with frescoes representing the Last Judgment done by Giorgio Vasari and Federico Zuccari at the end of the 16th century. In the niches of the pillars supporting the dome are statues of the Apostles.

The central chapel is home to the **Sarcophagus of San Zanobius** that contains the saint's relics. When you've finished wandering through the cathedral and admiring the art and stained glass windows, you can go to the top of the Duomo and get some great views of Florence. The way up is a little tiring, but the photo opportunities are fabulous.

Mercato Centrale
Via dell Ariento
Open Mon-Fri, 7am-2pm and 4pm-8pm, Sat 7am-12:15pm and 1pm-5pm, Sun 3pm-5pm.

Located in a building in the midst of the outdoor Mercato di San Lorenzo, the Mercato Centrale is Florence's main food market for fish, fresh meat, vegetables, cheeses, oils, breads, and many other delicacies. Don't think of leaving without having a sandwich at **Nerbone's**, a truly authentic Florentine experience. If you want to buy some salami or cheese the best purveyor of these treats is **Perini**.

Palazzo Vecchio
Piazza della Signoria
www.palazzovecchio.it
Open Mon-Fri 9am-7pm, and Sun 8am-1pm. Closed Sat. Admission: €5 for upstairs galleries.

The most imposing structure in the square is the **Palazzo Signoria**. Its construction began in the late 13th century and took hundreds of years to finish. In front of the building on the platform at the top of the steps, where the replica statue of *David* by Michelangelo now resides, orators used to harangue crowds, and for this reason this section of the building is called *Arringhiera* (The Haranguing Area). Located here are the *Marzocco* (a lion symbolizing the Florentine Republic; a stone copy of the original sits in the National Museum); *Judith and Holofernes* created by Donatello in 1460, which is a record of the victory over the Duke of Athens; and *Hercules and Cacus* created by Baccio Bandinelli.

The interior is mainly filled with artwork glorifying the Medici family, who ruled the Florentine Republic for centuries. Everything is elaborate and ornate, as befitting the richest family in the world at that time.

Piazza della Signoria
This piazza, with the Palazzo, the Loggia, the fountain, the replica of the statue of David, the cafes and *palazzi* is incomparable in its beauty. Over the centuries great historical and political occurrences, as well as the lives of average Florentines, have all flowed through this piazza. This is a wonderful place to find a seat at a cafe and watch the people walk by.

The statue to the left of the Palazzo is Ammannati's Fountain with the giant figure of *Neptune*. Commonly called *Biancone* (Whitey) by the locals because of its bland appearance. Giambologna created the equestrian statue representing *Cosimo I dei Medici* on the left of the square.

Restaurant Tips

LA TERRAZZA
Rinascente, 5th Floor, Piazza della Repubblica 1, Tel. 055/ 283-612. Open 10am-8pm.
Shhh. Not many tourists know about this café that overlooks the the Duomo and the rest of Florence. Located on the roof of the Rinascente department store.

I FRATELLINI
Via dei Cimatori 38/r, Tel. 055/239-6096. Open noon-midnight.
A visit to Florence must include a stop at this hole in the wall wine bar. No bigger than six feet wide by 4 feet deep, it is still the heart and soul of Florentine nightlife.

Pitti Palace
Piazza dei Pitti
Tel. 055/287-096.
Building hours: Tue-Sat 9am-7pm.
Most museums only open until 2pm. Sun and Holidays 9am-1pm. Closed on Mon. Admission.

Built for the rich merchant Luca Pitti in 1440, based on a design by Filippo Brunelleschi. Currently it is divided into six different museums; and since the upkeep and security for this building is so expensive, each museum charges their own entrance fee.

The Museo degli Argenti *(www.sbas.firenze.it/argenti)* contains works in amber, ivory, silver, crystal, precious woods and enamel collected by the Medici and Lorraine families. Closed the 1st, 3rd, and 5th Mondays and 2nd and 4th Sundays of the month. Admission €6.

The Museo delle Porcelane *(www.sbas.firenze.it/argenti)* is situated in the Boboli Gardens and housed in a quaint little building near the Belvedere Fortress at the top of the hill. This porcelain collection reflects the taste of the Medici and the many families that resided in the Pitti Palace after the Medici's decline. The 1st, 3rd, and 5th Mondays and 2nd and 4th Sundays of the month closed. Admission €6 includes entrance to the Boboli Gardens.

The Galleria Palatina e Apartamenti Reali, also known as the Pitti Gallery, includes paintings, sculptures, frescoes and furnishings of the Medici and Lorraine families. This gallery has some fine works from the 16th and 17th centuries and the most extensive collection of works by Raphael anywhere in the world. Other artists included here are Andrea del Sarto, Fra' Bartolomeo, Titian and Tintoretto, Velasquez, Murillo, Rubens, Van Dyke and Ruisdal. For more info: *www.sbas.firenze.it/palatina.*

The royal apartments feature an elaborate display of furnishings, carpets, wonderful silks covering the walls, as well as some fine paintings collected and displayed by the house of Savoy – the most notable of which is a series of portraits of the family of Louis XV of France. Admission €6 includes entrance to the Museo delle Carozze.

The Museo delle Carozze *(www.sbas.firenze.it/palatina)* houses carriages used by the court of the houses of Lorraine and Savoy when they ruled Florence.

The Galleria d'Arte Moderna *(www.sbas.firenze.it/gam)* occupies thirty rooms on the second floor of the palace and offers a thorough introduction to Italian painting from neo-classicism to 1945. The 1st, 3rd, and 5th Mondays and 2nd and 4th Sundays of the month closed. Admission €4 includes entrance to the Galleria del Costume.

The Galleria del Costume *(www.sbas.firenze.it/gam)* contains clothing from the 16th century to modern day.

Ponte Vecchio

Literally meaning Old Bridge, the name came about because the bridge has been around since Etruscan times. The present bridge was rebuilt on the old one in the 14th century by Neri di Fiorvanti. Thankfully this beautiful bridge with its gold and silver shops was spared the Allied and Axis bombardments during World War II. In the middle of the bridge are two arched openings that offer wonderful views of the Arno. On the downstream side of the bridge is a bust of Benvenuto Cellini, a Renaissance goldsmith and sculptor, done by Raphaele Romanelli in 1900.

Santa Croce
Piazza Santa Croce
Tel. 055/246-6105
Open 10am-12:30pm and 2:30pm-6:30pm (3-5pm in off-season). Closed Wed. Admission: €4.

The church of Santa Croce sits in the Piazza Santa Croce, surrounded by ancient palazzi. In this piazza, on any night, when all the shops are closed, you will feel as if you've stepped back into the Renaissance. In the center of the square is a statue of Dante Aligheri, he of *Divine Comedy* fame. The church itself is ornate yet simple and is part of the Franciscan Order.

Construction was begun in 1295 but its modern facade was created in 1863. It has a slim bell tower whose Gothic style doesn't seem to fit with this modern exterior. The interior, on the other hand, fits perfectly with the simple stonework of the bell tower.

Of the many Italian artistic, religious, and political geniuses that lie buried beneath Santa Croce, the most famous has to be that of Michelangelo himself.

Shopping Tips

SAN LORENZO MARKET
The most extensive daily market with the best products anywhere in Italy. Come here to buy your gifts and get some keepsakes to bring home.

VIA CALZAIUOLI
High-end shopping with many international stores and Italian boutiques.

VIA TOURNABUONI
Florence's equivalent to NYC's Fifth Avenue. Very high-end.

VIA DEL CORSO
Extending from the Piazza della Repubblica all the way over to the Santa Croce area, this is a great local shopping street.

Santa Maria Novella
Piazza Santa Maria Novella
Tel. 055/210-113
Closed Fri. Open 7am-11:30am and 3:30pm-6pm Mon-Thu and Sat, and Sun 3:30pm-5pm. Admission: €2.50.

Built in 1278 and completed in 1470, in the Gothic style with green and white marble decorations that are typically Florentine in character. To the left and right of the facade are tombs of illustrious Florentines all done in the same Gothic style.

As a young artist, Michelangelo worked on many of the amazing frescoes in the chapel of the high altar as a student. This is where he got his initial training that helped him paint the now famous frescoes in the Sistine Chapel in Rome. You can spend hours in here admiring these magnificent frescoes.

Uffizi Gallery
Piazzale degli Uffizi
Tel. 055/238-8651
www.sbas.firenze.it/uffizi; www.uffizi.firenze.it
Open Tue-Sat 8:30am-6:30pm, Sun and Holidays 9am-2pm.
Closed Mon. Admission: €6.50.

Note: reserve tickets in advance for a specific day and a
specific time of entry on the web through *www.firenze.net*
so that you do not have to stand in the incredibly long lines
common that occur at the Uffizi (and this holds true for the
Accademia and other heavily-touristed museums, especially in the summer). If you do not want to wait in the huge
line for general admission but have not reserved tickets in
advance on the web, go to door #2 and buy tickets for a
specific date and time in the future.

The building housing the Uffizi Gallery was begun in 1560
and was originally designed to be government offices, but
today holds the most important and impressive display of art
in Italy, and some would say the world. The gallery mainly
contains paintings of Florentine and Tuscan artists of the 13th
and 14th centuries, but you'll also find works from Venice,
Emilia, and other Italian art centers as well as Flemish, French,
and German studies. In conjunction there is a collection of
ancient sculptures.

These fabulous works of art were collected first by the Medici
family then later by the Lorraine family. The last of the Medici
donated the entire Gallery to the Tuscan state in 1737 so that
the rich collection gathered by her ancestors would never leave
Florence. If you want a complete listing of everyting in the
Uffizi, or an audio guided tour, you can get those as you enter.

Must-Sees at the Uffizi are:
• *Duke and Duchess of Urbino* - Piero della Francesca
• *Madonna of the Pomegranate, The Primavera, The Birth of
Venus,* and *Annunciation* - Botticelli
• *Madonna of the Goldfinch* - Raphael

- *Holy Family* - Michelangelo
- *Venus of Urbino* - Titian
- *Young Bacchus* - Caravaggio
- *Portrait of an Old Man and Two Self Portraits* - Rembrandt
- *Portrait of Isabelle Brandt* - Rubens

Another place to visit in the Uffizi is the Cafetteria Bartolini, located on the second floor. The food's not that great, but the view of the Palazzo Vecchio is great for photographs.

FLORENCE GETTING THERE/GETTING AROUND

Florence's Aeroporto Amerigo Vespucci (*www.airport.florence.it*) has an information desk in the arrival terminal open from 7:30am to 11:30pm everyday. The bus service is the best and least expensive way to get to Florence from the airport, but if you want to go by taxi, there is a taxi stand outside the main exit from the airport. €20. The SITA bus station is located next to the train station in Florence just off the Piazza della Stazione. Buses leave every half-hour between the bus station and the airport, starting at 5:30am until 11:00pm. It takes 25 minutes and costs €5. Major car rental companies are also represented at the airport.

LONDON

London is one of the world's most captivating cities and just oozes history and culture. You'll be bowled over by its fantastic museums and galleries, dazzling shops, pulsating nightlife, and glorious parks and gardens that make it the world's greenest capital. And let's not forget the pomp and pageantry that London is famous for—from the Changing of the Guard ceremony to the grand parades and processions of the City of London. Those with epicurean savvy will know that some of the world's finest chefs—and restaurants—are located here.

The Tower of London
Tower Hill, EC3
Tel. 0870 756 6060
Open Mon-Sat 9am-6pm, Sun 10am-6pm
Admission: £14.50
Nearest Tube: Tower Hill
www.hrp.org.uk

London's top visitor attraction is best known for its gory associations with many of the nation's most famous historical figures—Anne Boleyn and Sir Thomas More to name just a couple—and for the famous "Beefeaters" or yeomen of the guard, who double up as very informative and helpful tour guides. William the Conqueror, seeking to consolidate his new power base in London, built the 90-ft.-tall White Tower in 1078, its walls up to 15 ft. thick. Inside, there's a collection of armor since the time of Henry, and in the basement there's an exhibition of gruesome tools used in torture.

A more reflective atmosphere pervades the Chapel of St. John, on the second floor, pure and simple Norman in style. Close to the White Tower is another spiritual oasis: the Chapel of St. Peter ad Vincula, now fully restored to its Tudor glory, with a fine Spanish chestnut ceiling, and the tombs of Anne Boleyn, Catherine Howard and Sir Thomas More. Other must-see parts of the complex are the Bloody Tower, where the Little Princes (Edward V and the Duke of York) were allegedly murdered by their uncle, Richard II, and the Traitor's Gate, once the Tower's main entrance from the Thames. Tower Green, just north of the Tower and outside its walls, was the main mass execution site.

The incredible crown jewels are in the Jewel House, but be prepared for long lines—especially in summer. Among them, see the Imperial State Crown, made for Victoria's coronation in 1838.

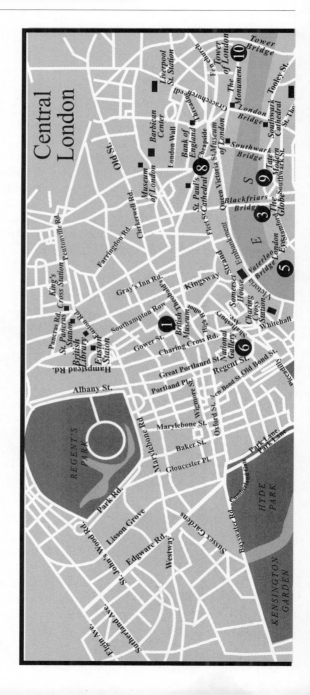

Central London

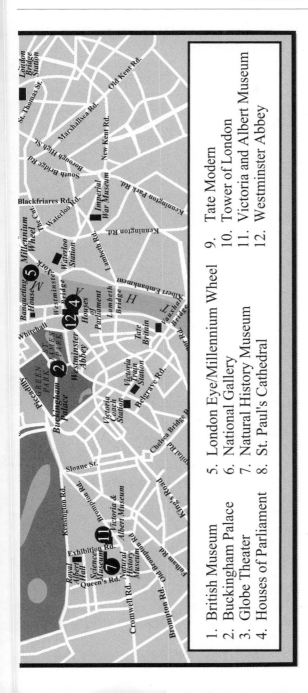

1. British Museum
2. Buckingham Palace
3. Globe Theater
4. Houses of Parliament
5. London Eye/Millennium Wheel
6. National Gallery
7. Natural History Museum
8. St. Paul's Cathedral
9. Tate Modern
10. Tower of London
11. Victoria and Albert Museum
12. Westminster Abbey

It has nearly 3,000 stones, mainly diamonds, including a priceless ruby worn by Henry V at the Battle of Agincourt in 1415. The Second Star of Africa, a 320-carat diamond, is also stunning, but even bigger is the First Star of Africa, the largest cut diamond in the world. It's part of the Sceptre with the Cross. If you're here at the right time, you might catch one of the Tower's ancient ceremonies, the 700-year-old Ceremony of the Keys.

St. Paul's Cathedral
St Paul's Churchyard, EC4
Tel 0207 246 8348
Open Mon to Sat 8:30am-4pm
Admission: £9
Nearest Tube: St Paul's
www.stpauls.co.uk

Completed in 1710, St Paul's dominates the City skyline. The Renaissance-style structure stretches over 500 ft. in length and 365 ft. from ground level to the top of the dome—a fitting scene for the royal wedding of Prince Charles to Lady Diana Spencer in 1981. The dome dominates the whole building. You can climb to the level of the Whispering Gallery, and higher still, to the Stone Gallery, for a spectacular 360-degree view of London.

Buckingham Palace
The Mall, SW1
Open Aug and Sep 9:30am-3:45pm; changing of the Guard ceremony 11:30am daily in the summer, alternate days in winter
Admission: £14
Nearest Tube: St James's Park
www.the-royal-collection.org.uk

The Queen's central London residence was originally built for the Duke of Buckingham, then purchased in 1762 by George III who needed space for his 15 children and courtiers. It has only housed the monarch since 1837, when Victoria transferred here from Kensington Palace. The Palace is 360 ft. long and contains 600 rooms, including the magnificent State Ballroom, scene of many glittering state banquets; Queen Victoria's

Picture Gallery, with paintings by Rembrandt, Van Dyck and Canaletto; and the Throne Room, with a pair of rather tacky pink chairs with the initials 'ER' and 'P'. The Queen and Prince Philip live in twelve rooms in the north wing. The Palace is not generally open to the public, but a small number of rooms are open in the summer.

Westminster Abbey
Dean's Yard, SW1
Tel. 0207 222 5152
Open Mon-Fri 9:20am-3:45pm, Sat 9am -1:45pm
Admission: £10 adults, £6 under 16.
Nearest Tube: Westminster
www.westminster-abbey.org

Saxon King Edward (later venerated as "the Confessor") founded the Abbey in 1065, when it was part of a Benedictine monastery. Harold was crowned king here in 1066, as was his vanquisher, William of Normandy, and just about every monarch since. It's very much the "national church," cluttered with tombs and monuments to the great and good. It's also been the setting for countless national events—the weddings and funerals of kings and queens, and, more recently, the moving funeral service for Diana, Princess of Wales. The twin towers at the west end were designed by Sir Christopher Wren, and added in the 17th century.

Entering by the west door, the nave, with its elegant rib-vaulting, spreads out before you as far as the intricately gilded choir screen. Beyond this lies one of the highlights of the Abbey, the Henry VII Chapel. Close to the main west door is the Tomb of the Unknown Warrior, an anonymous World War I soldier, while just a few paces away is the marble memorial to Sir Winston Churchill; his funeral service took place here in 1965. Pass through into the choir area, with its 19th-century stalls, and into the North Transept. The Rose Window here is one of the largest in Britain.

To proceed into the Henry VII Chapel and beyond, you'll need to pay an additional admission charge, but it's worth it.

The Chapel, with more fine rib-vaulting, carvings and sculptures, has been described as "the finest in Christendom." Here, you can see the white marble tomb of Elizabeth I, buried with her half-sister Mary I. Further on is the Chapel of Edward the Confessor and the Coronation Chair, where many monarchs have been crowned. Another focal point for visitors is Poets' Corner, with monuments to just about every British literary luminary starting with Chaucer. Other Abbey attractions worth at least a peep are the 13th-century Chapter House, and the Museum, located in the Norman undercroft.

The Houses of Parliament
Parliament Square, SW1
Tel. 0870 906 3773
Hours vary, depending on when parliament is in session. Guided tours during summer recess early Aug to late Sep Mon-Sat 9:15am-7:30pm
Admission (tour): £5
Nearest Tube: Westminster
www.parliament.uk

Just across the road from Westminster Abbey are the Houses of Parliament, dwarfed by the 363 ft.-high St. Stephen's Tower and Big Ben—not the name of the clock, but of the bell that strikes the hour.

The National Gallery
Trafalgar Square, WC2
Tel. 0207 747 2885
Open daily 10am-6pm
Admission: Free
Nearest Tube: Charing Cross
www.nationalgallery.org.uk

Occupying one side of Trafalgar Square, the neo-Classical National Gallery houses one of the world's most comprehensive collections

Restaurant Tip

IVY
1 West Street, WC2
Tel 020 7836 4751
Nearest Tube:
Leicester Square
Classic British dishes like braised beef in stout, and haddock and chips (with mushy peas) prevail, with more contemporary options too. Expensive.

of western paintings, the history of art from the 13th to the 20th century. Among the earliest works, the Wilton Diptych (French

School, late-14th century) is the greatest treasure. It shows Richard II being introduced to the Madonna and Child by John the Baptist and Saxon King Edward the Confessor (founder of Westminster Abbey).

Italian art, much of which you'll find in the Sainsbury Wing, is represented by Masaccio, della Francesca, da Vinci, Michelangelo, a roomful of Raphaels with the breathtaking *Crucifixion* as a centerpiece, and notable works by Titian, Tintoretto and Veronese. Northern Europe is also well represented, including Breughel's *Adoration* and Vermeer's *Young Woman at a Virginal*. And there's a roomful of Rembrandts—including four stunning portraits—a roomful of Rubens, Van Dyke's massive and famous painting of an equestrian Charles I, as well as works by some of the greatest British artists—Constable, Turner, Reynolds, Gainsborough and Hogarth.

Spanish art is represented by Velesquez, El Greco, and Goya, while other rooms are dedicated to French painters, such as Delacroix and Ingres, 19th-century Impressionists like Manet, Monet and Renoir, and Post-Impressionists like Cezanne and Van Gogh.

The Natural History Museum
Cromwell Road, SW7
Tel 0207 942 5000
Open Mon-Sat 10am-5:50pm, Sun 11am-5:50pm
Admission: free
Nearest Tube: South Kensington
www.Nhm.ac.uk

This massive Victorian cathedral of natural history is the most visited of all the London museums. You'll be met by a huge 80-ft.-long, 150-million-year-old diplodocus dinosaur, surrounded by glass cases containing fossils of various creatures—such as lions, elephants and bears—associated with Africa and Asia today, but which millions of years ago roamed where you're now standing. Kids (but maybe not mom) will love the Creepy Crawlies Gallery, with its gigantic enlarged scorpion and a host of cuddly taratulas, and everyone will be thrilled by the Earth Galleries, where, among other things, you can see a mock-up of a shop damaged during the 1995 earthquake at Kobe, Japan.

The British Museum
Great Russell Street, WC1
Tel 0207 323 8920
Open daily 10am-5:30pm, Thu and Fri until 8:30pm
Admission: Free
Nearest Tube: Holborn, Tottenham Court Road
www.thebritishmuseum.ac.uk

The mind-blowing British Museum contains one of the most extensive collections of art and artifacts in the world. There are antiquities from Egypt, Western Asia, Greece and Rome; Prehistoric and Romano-British, Medieval Renaissance, Modern and Oriental collections; prints, drawings—some six-and-a-half-million items, ranging from fragments of ancient manuscripts to colossal statues, spread out over 13 acres.

As you enter the front hall, check out the Assyrian Transept, the winged and human-headed bulls and lions that once

Restaurant Tips

LE PALAIS DU JARDIN
136 Long Acre, WC2
Tel 020 7379 5353
Nearest Tube: Covent Garden
Noisy, trendy brasserie and seafood bar. The menu includes seafood, venison, confit of duck, and, good heavens, bangers and mash. Moderate.

CHELSEA KITCHEN
98 King's Road, SW3
Tel. 0207 589 1330
Nearest Tube: Sloane Square
No-frills restaurant where you can get a two- or three-course meal for well under £10. As you'd expect, it's very basic—pasta, omelettes, stews ... Inexpensive.

guarded the gateways to the palaces of Assyrian kings. Nearby is the **Black Obelisk of Shalmaneser III**, depicting Jehu, King of Israel, paying tribute. From here you can access the hall of Egyptian sculpture and see the famous **Rosetta Stone**, whose discovery paved the way to the decoding of hieroglyphics. Also on the ground floor is the **Duveen Gallery**, where you'll find the **Elgin Marbles**, the **Manuscripts Room**, with an amazing range of manuscripts of every kind—Dickens' handwritten draft of *Nicholas Nickelby*, the original manuscripts of several Beatles' songs, Handel's *Messiah*, an original **Magna Carta**, a 15th-century edition of Chaucer's *Canterbury Tales*, and the famous **Gutenburg Bible** of 1455.

On the second floor are the galleries of the Department of Medieval and Later Antiquities. One of the most interesting exhibits here is the remains of an **Anglo-Saxon burial ship**, containing gold jewelry, armor, weapons, silverware and other implements. The main attractions of the upper floor are the **Egyptian Antiquities**, the largest and most comprehensive collection outside Cairo. **Room 63** is magnificent, looking like a set from *The Mummy*.

Tate Modern
Located at Bankside, SE1
Tel 020 7887 8888
Open Sun-Thu 10am-6pm, Fri-Sat 10am-10pm
Admission: Free, but donation welcome
Nearest Tune: Blackfriars or Southwark

Modern art from 1900 to the present, housed in a stunningly converted former power station. The emptied-out former Turbine Hall runs the length of the building, and is now the setting for temporary exhibits. From here, you're swept up by escalator through two floors featuring a café, shops and auditorium to three levels of galleries. Among the amazing collection of pieces on display are works by Bacon, Dali, Matisee, Picasso and Warhol.

The London Eye (Millennium Wheel)
Jubilee Gardens, SE1
Tel. 0870 500 0600

Open daily Oct-May 10am-8pm (June-Sep until 9pm)
Admission: £13, children £6.50
Nearest Tube: Westminster
www.ba-londoneye.com

This huge, 450-ft.-high ferris wheel—the largest of its kind in the world—has become one of London's most popular tourist attractions since opening in 2000. The wheel moves extremely slowly (one revolution takes around 20 minutes), affording passengers spectacular views of the whole city and beyond. It's a great place to start your London visit.

Windsor Castle
Brewhouse Yard, Windsor, Berkshire
Tel. 0175 383 1118
Open Nov-Feb 9:45am-4:15pm (last admission 3pm); Mar-Oct 9:45am-5:15pm (last admission 4pm)
Admission: Adults £13.50, seniors £12, under 17 £7.50, under 5 free.
Windsor is best accessed by train from London Waterloo (about 35 minutes).
www.royal.gov.uk

Windsor Castle was built 900 years ago by William the Conqueror to guard the western approaches to London. Today Windsor Castle is still a working palace, and the State Apartments contain some of the finest works of art, armor, paintings and decor in the world. Large sections of the Castle that were razed to the ground during the disastrous fire of 1992 have been completely rebuilt and refurbished to the highest

Shopping Tip

HARRODS
87-135 Brompton Road, SW1, Tel. 0207 730 1234
Open Mon-Sat 10am to 7pm. Closed Sun
Nearest Tube: Knightsbridge
www.harrods.co.uk

The world's most famous department store, established in 1849, is a massive, 15-acre six-story Edwardian terracotta pile, illuminated at night by thousands of white lights. The store's motto is *Omnia, omnibus, ubique* (Latin for "everything, for everyone, everywhere"). Most visitors make a beeline for the legendary Food Hall, with its stunning art nouveau tiling and unbelievable displays of fish, meat and vegetables and breads.

standards, such as the Grand Reception Rooms, the Green and Crimson Drawing Rooms and the State and Octagonal Dining Rooms. The Queen gives lavish banquets in St. George's Hall, which had its ancient roof completely destroyed; today a brand-new roof covers the 600-year-old hall.

Check out St. George's Chapel, dating from the 15th and 16th centuries, with its superb fan vaulting and beautifully carved choir stalls. Don't miss the State Apartments, lavish beyond belief, with priceless antiques, Gobelin tapestries, old master paintings and even a Louis XVI bed. Also here are the Throne Room and the Waterloo Chamber, where you can examine paintings of Napoleon's foes. Several items of armor are on show, and you can take a look at the superb Queen's Collection of Master Drawings, with works by Leonardo, and 87 Holbein portraits.

You should also take a look at Queen Mary's Dolls' House, left of the entrance to the State Apartments. Sir Edward Lutyens won the commission to create the Dolls' House in 1921. It was built on a scale of one to twelve, and involved over 1,500 craftsmen. At Windsor you can also see (another) Changing of the Guard ceremony. This takes place daily (except Sundays) at 11am from April to the end of June, and on alternate days at other times of the year. Call *0175 386 8286* to confirm the times.

Hampton Court Palace
East Molesey
Tel. 0870 752 7777
State Apartments open Apr-Oct Tue-Sun 9:30am-6pm; Nov-Mar Tue-Sun 9:30am-4:30pm, Monday 10:15-4:30pm
Admission: Adults £12, children £8. Grounds open 8am-dusk daily (free, but maze £4)
Take a train from Waterloo to Hampton Court Station (about 35 minutes)
www.hrp.org.uk

This magnificent red-brick Tudor house 20 miles west of central London was begun in 1514 by the powerful Lord Chancellor, Cardinal Wolsey. His desire to create the most lavish palace in the land upset Henry VIII so much that Wolsey felt obliged to give it to the king, and Henry moved in in 1525. Henry made some additions, including the Great Hall and Chapel. Greater expansion took place during the reign of William and Mary, when Sir Christopher Wren was commissioned to extend the Palace to the rear, resulting in the very beautiful South Wing. Start your visit at Henry's Great Hall, designed to make you feel small and intimidated. Its 60-ft. walls are covered with Flemish tapestries dating from 1540, illustrating the history of Abraham. The Great Kitchen has been painstakingly restored. In Henry's day it would have had a staff of over 200 men, women and children.

The Royal Chapel is another part of the original Tudor building that remains virtually intact, but with additions by Wren and a reredos screen carved by Grinling Gibbons. There's a superb turquoise-and-gold fan-vaulted ceiling painted by Sir James Thornhill. To the left and right of Wren's Fountain Court are the King's and Queen's Apartments. The King's Guard Chamber is decorated as it was in 1699, with a display of 3,000 arms arranged in decorative patterns. The Privy Chamber was out of bounds to all but the Groom of the Stool (you can guess which stool this is). The highlight here is a beautiful ceiling illustrating Endymion asleep in the arms of Morpheus. The palace is full of priceless paintings, original furniture and—it's said—the ghost of Catherine Howard, protesting her innocence of the adultery that had her beheaded.

Outside, explore the gardens, or visit the famous Hampton Court Maze. And don't miss the Renaissance Picture Gallery, with a collection of works by Holbein, Titian and Breughel's *Massacre of the Innocents*.

Victoria and Albert Museum
Cromwell Road, SW7
Tel 0870 906 3883
Open daily 10am-5:45pm, Wed until 10pm
Admission: Adults £5, seniors £3, students and under 18 free
Nearest Tube: South Kensington
www.vam.ac.uk

This museum prides itself on being the largest and most influential decorative arts museum in the world, its 146 galleries showcasing such varied fields as ceramics, sculpture, furniture, jewelry and textiles. This visually stunning Gothic building also contains the National Collections of sculpture, glass, ceramics, watercolors, portrait miniatures and photographs, and houses the National Art Library. Among the museum's many treasures are the 12th-century Eltinberg Reliquary, the early English Gloucester candlestick, ands the Syon cope, a priceless vestment woven in England in the 14th century.

Kew Gardens
Kew Road, Kew Surrey
Tel 0208 940 1171
Gardens open daily 9:30am-6:30pm. Glasshouses Mar-Oct 9:30am-5:30pm, Nov-Feb 9:30am-4:15pm
Admission: £11.75
Nearest Tube: Kew
www.rbgkew.org.uk

It's often forgotten that The Royal Botanical Gardens at Kew, in west London, are a major botanical research institute, containing more than 38,000 plant species in over 300 acres of public parkland. The Gardens were founded by Queen Caroline and Princess Augusta in the 18th century. Rapid expansion took place in the next century, when some of the huge glasshouses were built, containing all kinds of exotic species, many of them quite rare. The metal and glass Palm House, built in 1848, contains, as the name implies, a wondrous collection of tropical foliage. The beautiful Water Lily House is also a must-see. A major storm destroyed most of the trees in 1987, the same year the Institute received a major boost with the opening of the ultramodern Princess of Wales Conservatory, housing plants in ten different computer-controlled time zones.

The grounds are also a popular attraction, especially Queen Charlotte's Cottage, a summerhouse used by George III and his wife Charlotte, who died here in 1818. The 10-story-high Great Pagoda, built in 1762 by William Chambers, is another star attraction, and the newly restored Kew Palace, built in 1631 as the Dutch House, was once a favored royal residence of George III.

The Globe Theatre
21 New Globe Walk, SE1
Tel. 0207 902 1400 (Theater performance information: 020 7401 9919)
Open May-Sep daily 9am-noon; Oct-Apr 10am-5pm
Admission: Adults £9, seniors and students £7.50, children £6.50
Nearest Tube: London Bridge
www.shakespeares-globe.org

Pub Tip

SHERLOCK HOLMES
10 Northumberland Street, WC2
Tel 0207 930 2644
Nearest Tube: Charing Cross
This neighborhood pub was a frequent haunt of Sir Arthur Conan Doyle and features in his most famous tome, *The Hound of the Baskervilles.*

Shakespeare's original Globe was about 200 yards away from its replacement, which opened in 1996, thanks to the unstinting efforts of American actor Sam Wanamaker, after learning that there was no permanent memorial to the Bard in London. Authentic Elizabethan methods were used to build the theater, and the first thatched roof in London since the Great Fire was a fitting finishing touch. Plays are presented in natural light to up to 1,000 people seated on wooden benches and another 500 standing on a carpet of shells, as they did 400 years ago. The theater is open for performance only in the summer, but guided tours are available year round from the Globe Exhibition Centre next door.

LONDON GETTING THERE/GETTING AROUND

Most flights from North America arrive at either Heathrow, *www.baa.co.uk,* about 15 miles west of the city, or Gatwick, *www.baa.co.uk,* about 25 miles south.

The most expensive way to travel is the famous black cabs. The ride from Heathrow will cost somewhere around £35; from Gatwick, £45, and up. Mini cabs often operate a fixed rate—usually about £25—for travel into central London. Confirm the price before you start your journey. Some companies offer shuttle bus services from the airports direct to your hotel. Among the best are Airport Transfers *(Tel. 020 7403 2228)* and Hotelink *(Tel. 01293 532244)*, who charge £12 per person to the West End from Heathrow, and £18 from Gatwick. Tipping for all taxi drivers is customarily 10%. You can also go by train: the Heathrow Express *(Tel. 08456 001515)* runs up to four trains an hour from the Airport to Paddington Train Station. Fares start at around £13.

By bus, National Express *(Tel. 08705 757747)* run services from Victoria Bus Station and from King's Cross Train Station. Fares start at £10. By Underground, The Piccadilly Line connects Heathrow with central London. Trains run every five to ten minutes, and fares are £3.60 for adults, £1.50 for children. The ride into central London takes around 45 minutes, and costs £3.50.

The Underground (Tube) is by far the quickest way to get around London. Each of the 12 underground lines is color-coded. You'll need to know the final destination on your chosen line (which is marked on the front of the train and on the overhead illuminated display) and the general direction (north, south, east or west) that the train is traveling. It may sound complicated, but it won't take long to get the hang of it. Trains normally run from around 5am to midnight. Don't lose your ticket–or you might have to pay a hefty fine.

PLANNING YOUR TRIP

Airports/Arrival
See the final section in each individual destination.

Customs/Passports
Citizens of the US who have been away more than 48 hours can bring home $800 of merchandise duty-free every 30 days. For more information, go to Traveler Information ("Know Before You Go") at *www.customs.gov*. Canadians can bring back C$750 each year if they have been gone for 7 days or more. You'll need a valid passport to enter Europe.

Eating
When a service charge is added to your bill (and it almost always is), no tip is usually expected. Exceptions to the rule exist in France, Germany, and the Netherlands, where it's expected that you will either leave your small change or round up the bill to an even amount. Remember that waiters, just as in the US and Canada, greatly appreciate tips.

Restaurant prices in this book are for a main course and without wine:
• Inexpensive: under €10
• Moderate: €11-€20
• Expensive: €21-€30
• Very Expensive: over €30

Note: In London, prices are £.

The author of this book is the co-author of *Eating & Drinking in Paris*, *Eating & Drinking in Italy* and *Eating & Drinking in Spain*. These pocket books have extensive menu translators to help you decipher menus in French, Italian and Spanish. You can order them online either through www.openroadguides.com or www.eatndrink.com.

Electricity
The electrical current in Europe is 220 volts as opposed to 110

volts found at home. Don't fry your electric razor, hairdryer or laptop. You'll need a converter and an adapter. Some laptops don't require a converter, but why are you bringing them on vacation anyway?

Embassies/Consulates
Below are the addresses and phone numbers for US embassies and consulates:
- Amsterdam: *19 Museumplein, Tel. 020/5755309*
- Barcelona: *23 Passeig Reina Elisenda, Tel. 932802227*
- Berlin: *4-5 Neustädtische Kirchstrasse, Tel. 030/83050*
- Florence: *38 Lungaro Vespucci, Tel. 055266951*
- London: *24 Grosvenor Square, Tel. 0274999000*
- Madrid: *75 Calle Serrano, Tel. 915872240 and 915872200*
- Marseille (Provence): *place Varian-Fry, tel. 04/91.55.92.00*
- Nice (Provence): *7 avenue Gustave V 04/93.88.89.55*
- Paris: *2 rue St-Florentin Tel. 01/43.12.22.22 or 01/43.12.23.47 Rome: 199 Via Veneto, Tel. 06/46741*
- Venice: *1 Largo Donegani (Milan), Tel. 02/290351*

Hotels
This travel guide is for travelers who already know where they're staying, although it includes a short list of hotels for each destination on pages 152-153. One great way to truly experience life in a European city is to rent an apartment. They're usually less expensive and larger than a hotel room. There are many apartments for rent on the Internet. Try *www.rentalo.com.*

Insurance
Check with your health-care provider. Most policies don't cover you overseas. If that's the case, you may want to obtain medical insurance. You may also want to purchase trip-cancellation insurance; for insurance coverage, check out *www.insuremytrip.com.*

Language
If you make the effort to speak a little of the language of the country you're visiting, it will get you a long way. Even if all you can say is "Do you speak English?"
- French: Parlez-vous anglais? (*par-lay voo ahn-glay*)

- German: Sprechen Sie Englisch? (*shprehkh-ehn zee ehng-lish*)
- Spanish: Habla usted Inglés? (*ah-blah oos-tehd een-glehs*)
- Dutch: Spreekt U Engels? (*spraykt ou eng-els*)
- Italian: Parla Inglese? (*par-la een-glay-zay*)

It's common courtesy throughout Europe to greet a storekeeper when entering and say goodbye when leaving.

Maps
The maps in this book are meant to give you an overview of the sights in this book. Upon arrival, head to the tourist information center (there's one at every major airport) and get an inexpensive (or free) map of the city or area.

Mealtimes
In Europe, lunch is generally served from noon to around 2pm, and dinner from 8pm to 11pm. However, dining in Amsterdam is early and in Spain very late. Generally, the restaurant will be less crowded the earlier you get there. Make reservations!

Money
The euro (€) is the currency of the destinations in this guide except London, where they use the British pound (£). Before you leave for Europe, it's a good idea to get some local currency. It makes your arrival a lot easier. Call your credit-card company or bank before you leave to tell them that you'll be using your ATM or credit card outside the country. Many have automatic controls that can "freeze" your account if the computer program determines that there are charges outside your normal area. ATMs (with fees, of course) are the easiest way to change money in Europe. You'll find them everywhere. You can still get traveler's checks, but why bother?

Packing
Never pack prescription drugs, eyeglasses or valuables. Carry them on. Think black. It always works for men and women. Oh, and by the way, pack light. Don't ruin your trip by having to lug around huge suitcases.

Public Transportation

Parking is chaotic, gas is extremely expensive, and driving in Europe's main cities is an unpleasant "adventure." With the incredible public-transportation system, there's absolutely no reason to rent a car. If you drive to your hotel, park it and leave it there and use public transportation or your feet. From the métro in Paris to the U-Bahn in Berlin, learn to use public transportation. It will make you feel like a local and will save you tons of money. Travel within and between European countries by rail is easy and economical. Try *www.raileurope.com* to purchase a Eurail pass (good in 17 countries) and single-country passes.

Restrooms

There aren't a lot of public restrooms. If you need to go, your best bet is to head (no pun intended) to the nearest café. It's considered good manners to purchase something if you use the restroom.

Safety

Don't wear a fanny pack; it's a sign that you're a tourist and an easy target (especially in crowded tourist areas). Avoid wearing expensive jewelry. Don't leave valuables in your car.

Taxes

Hotels and restaurants are required by law to include taxes and service charges. Value Added Tax (VAT) up to 20%, higher on some luxury goods, is included in the price of merchandise (except services such as restaurants). Check *www.globalrefund.com* for the latest information on refunds (and help for a fee).

Telephone

• Calling the US or Canada from Europe: Dial 00 (wait for the tone), dial 1 plus the area code and seven-digit local number
• Calling from US or Canada to Europe: Dial 011, plus the country code, plus the area code and local number. Remember that when dialing France, you drop the 0 in the area code.

The country codes for the destinations in this book are:
• France 33
• Germany 49

- Netherlands 31
- Spain 49
- UK 44
- Italy 39.

Phone cards are the cheapest way to call.

Time
When it's noon in New York City, it's 6pm in the cities in this book except for London, which is an hour earlier. For hours of events or schedules, Europeans use the 24-hour clock. So 6am is 0600 and 1pm is 1300.

Tipping
See the "Eating" section above for restaurant tipping. Other tips: 10% for taxi drivers, €1 for room service, €1.50 per bag to the hotel porter, €1.50 per day for maid service, and €0.50 to bathroom attendants.

Walks
The walks in this book are designed to take one to two hours (except as otherwise noted). If you choose to visit the museums along the way, your walks can last much longer.

Water
Tap water is safe in Europe. If you have a sensitive stomach, buy bottled water.

Web Sites
- Amsterdam: *www.amsterdam.nl*
- Berlin: *www.berlin.de/English*
- London: *www.visitlondon.com*
- French Tourist Office: *www.franceguide.com*
- Italian Tourist Office: *www.italiantourism.com*
- Spain Tourist Office: *www.spain.info*
- US State Department: *http://travel.state.gov*

Weather
Before you leave for Europe, check out *www.weather.com*. July and August, the peak months for travel, are sunniest. May, June, September and October are the best months to travel.

Suggested Hotel List
Prices for two people in a double room
Expensive (over €200) ***
Moderate (€125 to €200) **
Inexpensive (under €100) *
In London, prices are £

BARCELONA
*** **Casa Camper,** *11 Carrer Elisabets, Tel. 93/3426280,
www.casacamper.com*
** **Hostal d'Uxelles,** *688 Gran Vía de les Corts Catalanes,
Tel. 93/2652560, www.hotelduxelles.com*
* **Hostal Girona,** *24 Carrer Girona, Tel. 93/2650259,
www.hostalgirona.com*

MADRID
*** **Quo,** *4 Calle Sevilla, Tel. 91/5329049,
www.hotelquopuertadelsol.com*
** **Hotel Carlos V,** *5 Calle Maestro Vitoria, Tel. 91/
5314100, www.bestwestern.es/hotelcarlosv.html*
* **7 Colors,** *14 Calle Huertas, Tel. 91/4296935,
www.7colorsrooms.com*

PARIS
*** **Jeu de Paume,** *54 rue St-Louis-en-l'Ile, Tel. 01/
43.26.14.18, www.jeudepaumehotel.com*
** **Jardins du Luxembourg,** *5 impasse Royer-Collard, Tel.
01/40.46.08.88, www.hotel-luxembourg.com*
* **Hôtel du Champ de Mars,** *7 rue du Champ de Mars, Tel.
01/45.51.52.30, www.hotel-du-champ-de-mars.com*

PROVENCE
*** **Château Eza,** *Rue de la Pise in Eze, Tel: 04/93.41.12.24,
www.chateaueza.com*
** **Les Olivettes,** *Ave. Henri Bosco (off of route 27) in
Lourmarin, Phone: 04/90.68.03.52. www.olivettes.com*
* **Hôtel de l'Amphithéâtre,** *5-7 rue Diderot in Arles, Phone:
04/90.96.10.30, www.hotelamphitheatre.fr*

AMSTERDAM
*** **Dylan,** *384 Keizersgracht, Tel. 020/530-2010,
www.dylanamsterdam.com*

** **Eden**, 144 Amstel, Tel. 020/530-7878, *www.bestwestern.nl*
* **Agora**, *462 Singel, Tel. 020/627-2200, www.hotelagora.nl*

BERLIN

*** **Adlon**, *77 Unter den Linden, Tel. 1-800-426-3135 (toll free), Tel. 22610, www.hotel-adlon.de*

** **Luisenhof**, *92 Köpenicker Strasse, Tel. 2462810, www.luisenhof.de*

* **Bogota**, *45 Schlüterstrasse, Tel. 8815001, www.hotelbogota.de*

VENICE

*** **Hotel Concordia**, *Calle Larga-San Marco 367, Tel. 041.5206866, www.hotelconcordia.com*

** **Agli Alboretti**, *Rio Terrà Foscarini-Dorsoduro 884, Tel. 041/5230058, www.aglialboretti.com*

* **Ca' San Marcuola**, *Campo San Marcuola-Cannaregio 1763, Tel. 041/716048, www.casanmarcuola.com*

ROME

*** **Barocco**, *Piazza Baberini 9, Tel. 06/487-2001, wwwhotelbarocco.com*

** **Locarno**, *Via della Penna 22, Tel. 06/361-0841, www.hotellocarno.com.*

* **Parlamento**, *Via della Convertite, Tel. 06/6992-1000, www.hotelparlamento.it*

FLORENCE

*** **Beacci-Tornabuoni**, *Via Tornabuoni 3, Tel. 055/212-645, www.bthotel.it*

** **La Scaletta**, *Via Guicciardini 13, Tel. 055/283-028, www.lascaletta.com*

* **Firenze**, *Piazza dei Donati 4 (off of Via del Corso), Tel. 055/268-301, www.hotelfirenze-fi.it*

LONDON

*** **Claridges**, *Brook Street, W1, Tel. 0207 499 2210, www.claridges.co.uk*

** **Durrant's**, *George Street, W1, Tel 0207 935 8131, www.durrantshotel.co.uk*

* **James House**, *108 Ebury Street, SW1, Tel 0207 730 7338, www.jamesandcartref.co.uk*

INDEX